Robert's Rules *of* Writing

SECOND EDITION

111 Unconventional Lessons That Every Writer Needs to Know

Robert Masello

ALLWORTH PRESS
NEW YORK

Allworth Press books may be purchased in bulk at special discounts for sales promotion, corporate gifts, fund-raising, or educational purposes. Special editions can also be created to specifications. For details, contact the Special Sales Department, Allworth Press, 307 West 36th Street, 11th Floor, New York, NY 10018 or info@skyhorsepublishing.com.

25 24 23 22 21   5 4 3 2 1

Published by Allworth Press, an imprint of Skyhorse Publishing, Inc. 307 West 36th Street, 11th Floor, New York, NY 10018. Allworth Press® is a registered trademark of Skyhorse Publishing, Inc.®, a Delaware corporation.

www.allworth.com

Cover design by Mary Ann Smith

Library of Congress Cataloging-in-Publication Data is available on file.

Print ISBN: 978-1-62153-783-0
eBook ISBN: 978-1-62153-784-7

Printed in the United States of America

CONTENTS

PREFACE

If ever there was a time when the world was in need of good writing—when it was clamoring for clear and convincing prose—that time is now. And that goes for everything from magazine articles to memoirs, short stories to blog columns, novels to screenplays. We're inundated with misinformation and disinformation, "fake news" bulletins and "alternative facts" (heretofore known as lies) and unending political spin from a bunch of bloviating dopes on TV. The academics are just as bad, turning normal human discourse into minefields across which no mere mortal dare tread. There are stories in literary quarterlies that even I, an English major from a fine old college, cannot begin to figure out and poems so inscrutable they positively scare me. Not to mention the endless proliferation of books that purport to teach anyone to write—I swear, if one more person ever says to me, "Hey, if you can talk, you can write," my head is going to explode—all of them written by people who can't write anything *but* advice for other writers.

So where do I get the nerve to add yet another book on writing to the already groaning shelf? Well, call it hubris, call it the need to unburden myself after a long and reasonably successful run at this, call it the altruistic desire to impart what I've learned the hard way after writing over twenty novels and nonfiction books, thousands of articles and essays for major magazines and newspapers, and episodes of popular TV shows that I myself, to be perfectly frank, would never have watched. (If you really feel the need to know more, you can read the About the Author page at the end of this book, where I name names, list credits, and disclose the details of my checkered past, all in an effort to assist my future biographers.)

What I'm *not* going to try to do in this book is untangle the thorny knots of grammatical construction ("a dependent clause can only take the subjunctive case when preceded by a dangling participle"), nor am I planning to offer a cheerleading session, assuring you that every word you write is a pearl. (Mine aren't, either.) This is instead a kind of tough love, the distillation of all the rules that professional writers, those of us who do this for what passes for a living, have figured out over the years—the straight and simple rules that address and smooth over the routine difficulties that we all face, whether we're working on a mystery novel or a movie script, a personality profile or a first-person essay, a magazine piece or an epic poem. Some of these rules, let me warn you, are provocative, controversial, counterintuitive. You may even want to duke it out with me over some of them, and that's okay, since you don't know where I live. (I hope.)

But you've just got to trust me when I say that these rules have proven themselves over time to be of great, practical use to many writers of all stripes and all abilities. I know that they have been to me.

Which is why I'm calling them—wait for the big reveal—*Robert's Rules of Writing.*

RULE 1.

BURN YOUR JOURNAL.

Just about every writing book I know says writing is a muscle that you have to regularly exercise and keep in use, and that if you don't know what to write, you shouldn't let that stop you. You should just start keeping a journal and writing down, at random, all your thoughts and ideas.

In *my* book—this one to be exact—that's almost always an immense waste of time and paper. The only muscle you'll be exercise by keeping a journal is your hand, and for that you'd be better off jumping rope.

If you feel like keeping a journal—something that neither you nor anyone else on earth will ever want to read—by all means be my guest.

But if you want to write something that may eventually see the light of day, that a magazine might buy, a publisher publish, or a producer produce, then you'll have to knock off the journaling and do the grunt work that real writing requires.

Nine out of ten struggling writers get stuck right there. Instead of confronting all the very real problems that any book or article or story poses, they retreat to those blasted journals, on the theory that they're loosening up their artistic tendons and free-associating their way to fresh ideas.

All they're really doing is keeping the manufacturers of those fancy blank books, the ones that uselessly clutter up the shelves at your local bookstores, in business.

All too often, writing in a journal is just a stall, a waiting game, a way to tell yourself that you're working when you're not, that you're doing something of value when you're just using up paper, that you're a writer when in fact you're just going through the motions of one. *Look at me! I had blank paper in front of me—and now it's filled with words!*

Anyone can do that. Anytime.

The *hard* part of writing isn't scribbling words on a page. The hard part is scribbling words that *mean* something, that make sense, that

build a narrative or lay out an argument, that construct a scene or articulate a position. It's not about how many pages you can cover with ink
in a day. In some cases, a good day's work might be a couple of paragraphs. But if those two paragraphs are right, then they're a lot more
valuable than ten or twenty pages of idle burbling.

Writing takes deliberation and thought, craft and commitment.

If you're serious about writing, burn the journal, and get to work.

RULE 2.

GET A PEN PAL.

But I don't want you to think I'm too hard-hearted.

I know what it's like to be stuck, to have the urgent *desire* to write, but nothing particular to say just now. That's usually when those alluring journals come out.

But try this. Instead of writing the stream-of-consciousness twaddle that generally fills those blank pages, try this instead—write a letter, to a friend.

Writing has to have a purpose; it's meant to communicate *something*, to *someone*, and if you're not ready to write for the general public—many times we're not—then try writing for a very specific audience—one that you know will be happy to hear from you. (People are so astonished to get letters these days, you might want to send a text in advance to warn them that one is on the way, lest they keel over in shock.) If you must, you could even make your letter an e-mail, but there's something about the ephemerality of e-mails, or texts and tweets for that matter, that virtually cries out for sloppiness and imprecision. A good, old-fashioned letter, hand-scrawled or printed out on paper, will require you to think before you write, as well as permit you to edit and revise and amend.

All the things, in other words, that honest-to-God writing makes you do!

It'll also put you in touch with a lot of important things. For one, your ideal audience. Much of the time, writers are stuck because we can't figure out who we're writing for, or because we've started imagining our audience as an indifferent, even hostile, crowd—a bunch of critics just waiting to take their shot at us. Writing to a friend will remind you that there are nice folks out there, folks you like and who like you back, who would be delighted to hear what you have to say.

Writing a letter can also remind you, in case you'd forgotten, what it *is* that you actually have to say. Look and see what flows from your flying fingertips, or your scribbling pen. Are you seeking comfort for a broken heart? Are you telling a funny story about the perfectly awful job interview you just went on? Are you ranting about the next-door neighbors who barbecue meats of unknown origin? Whatever it is, *that's* what you're thinking about, *that's* what's on your mind. And, if you wanted to, that's what you could be writing about for others, too—the dismal job interview could work as a humor piece for a local paper, the cookout kings next door could become characters in a screenplay, the broken romance story might be right for the "Modern Love" column in the *New York Times* (though the odds of capturing that particular Holy Grail are, I'm told, astronomical. I have the rejection letters—oops, rejection emails—to prove it.)

But because you're writing now with a purpose and a person in mind—instead of just sprawling all over a journal—you're paying attention, the way you should, to everything from pace to clarity. You're writing to interest and even, with any luck, entertain the friend who's going to receive this letter in a few days. And secretly, you're looking forward to the reaction your words are going to get.

However limited it may be, writing a letter is a form of publication. Next time you can go after a bigger—and paying—crowd.

RULE 3.

THROW OUT YOUR THESAURUS.

How many times, when you're telling a story at a party, do you stop dead to search for a bigger, better, or more impressive word than the one you were just about to utter?

Unless you were determined to lose your audience, probably not very often.

So why would you do it when you're writing?

The best writing is the writing that flows naturally, and without delay or hesitation, from the mind of the writer. It's writing that appears to have come effortlessly (however much effort actually went into it behind the scenes). It's writing that sounds like its author—you—and that uses *your* rhythm, *your* sensibility, and *your* vocabulary.

The minute you pick up a thesaurus, you've muddied the waters. Into the clear running stream of your prose, you've introduced an oil slick. Nothing sticks out in a piece of prose like the words you've plucked from those long lists of synonyms, each one more obscure than its predecessor.

Thesaurus words are words you would never use on your own; the fact that you had to resort to the thesaurus just to find them proves it. They aren't words that come readily to your mind, or that rest comfortably in your working vocabulary. Suddenly, you start sounding pompous, or precious. It's as if you've swapped your customary Hawaiian shirts and shorts for a three-piece suit and a watch fob. If you think people won't notice the change, think again.

The voice you write in is the voice your reader hears, and, ideally, grows to trust. It's the voice the reader becomes accustomed to, the one that makes a sort of pact between the two of you. When you stop writing with your own words, the words that you would or could summon up on your own, then you break that pact and you propel the reader out of your world and straight into Mr. Roget's. It's no different than if you were writing fiction and you put into a character's mouth words that the character could never have conjured up on his own. If you wrote about a high fashion editor and had her barking like a short-order cook, or a stevedore sounding like a diplomat, you'd be shaking your reader's belief not only in the character, but in the entire fictional world that the character inhabits.

Whatever it is you want to say in your work, find a way to say it not in words you've borrowed for this special occasion, like some rental tuxedo, but in words you already own, words that are already hanging in your closet. Those are the words that you'll be most comfortable wearing and that your readers will recognize you in.

RULE 4.

ZIP THE LIP.

Ever notice how, when an interviewer asks an author about his next project, the author gets very evasive. "Oh, I'm just noodling with a couple of things right now," or "Well, I hate to jinx anything by talking about it too soon."

Take an important cue from this.

Professional writers know that the more you talk about something you're planning to write, the less likely it is that you'll ever write it.

A book is like a steam engine, and the more you talk about it, the more you lower the internal pressure that's needed to make the thing run. All the energy that should be going back into the book is being squandered in talk and dissipated in the air.

If people do ask what you're working on these days, it's perfectly all right to say you're taking a shot at a murder mystery, a biography, a memoir of your curious years as a button man for the mob, because if you try to dodge the question altogether, you'll look snooty—"Oh, look at Mr. Fancy Pants here, thinks he's too smart for the likes of us!"—or just plain rude.

But if you talk too much, you'll get into trouble. Either you'll start going on about the subject of your book until your friends are bored to tears—and trust me, they're bored in three minutes—or, and this is even more dangerous, you'll go on about it until you begin to get bored yourself. There's nothing like hearing a story told over and over again to take the zest out of it, for you and everybody else.

In every book you write, there will be things you discover only along the way, points you suddenly want to make, themes that slowly emerge, stories that take surprising turns. But the place to discover these things is on the page, as you write, rather than at some cocktail party where the best you can do is jot something down on a napkin and hope, when you fish the darn thing out of your pocket the next morning, that it isn't hopelessly smudged and illegible.

Carry the book you're writing in your imagination, but keep your mouth closed. That way, nothing that belongs to the book will escape— no image will fade from overexposure, no dialogue will become rote, and no shocking twist will lose its full impact. Sealed in its original container—your head—your work will retain all of its freshness and flavor.

RULE 5.

CALL OUT THE
THOUGHT POLICE.

If there's one question successful writers get asked at virtually every public event they attend, it's "Where do you get your ideas?"—as if they could tell you, "Oh yeah, there's this great little shop on the corner of Lexington and 23rd. But go early, because the best ideas are gone by ten."

Oh man, if only there were such a shop. The line would be around the block, and, frankly, I'd be camped out at the head of it.

No, the best place to get ideas—for articles, essays, books, stories, scripts—is much closer to home than that. It's your own head, if only you'll learn to pay proper attention to what's going on in there.

Sure, you can sit down with a legal pad in your lap, shut your eyes, press your hands to your temples, and bid the ideas to come. But that probably works as well as guessing the right lottery numbers. With something as ephemeral as ideas, intense concentration can sometimes prove to be more of an impediment than a help.

Meanwhile, all day long, everyday, great notions are flowing right by you, but just under your radar. Where are they? What are they? They're in the thoughts you're thinking as you drive to work, or as you sit on the bus observing your fellow passengers. They're crossing your mind while you have dinner with friends and somebody says something that makes you laugh. They're in the tub with you, as you lie back with your head on the cold porcelain rim, and wonder what your colleague really meant by that weird remark at work.

All day long, like a radio that's never turned off, your mind is broadcasting your interests, your obsessions, your worries, your fears, your deepest concerns, and these are the raw materials from which you will build your most effective work. They're the things that please and plague you, trouble and tempt you, the things that get your sympathies engaged, your temper aroused, your sense of humor tickled. But because you're doing something else at the time—because you're not actually in the working mode—you're not paying attention, and you're not giving these thoughts their due.

In fact, half the time you're trying to banish these thoughts—so what, for instance, if the third girlfriend in a row has just broken up with you for no reason you can discern? You tell yourself to forget about it, and think about something more constructive. Like your stock portfolio. But your thoughts, undoubtedly, keep returning to that sore point. What is it, you wonder, that women really want? Is it even remotely possible that you are doing something wrong? Should you *not* have suggested that she throw out everything in her closet and replace it all with those catalog items you'd so helpfully flagged with colorful Post-it notes? Was that . . . insensitive?

Here's your material, here's your mother lode. Here's something you feel strongly about, even if your chief emotion is confusion. And this is where you will find your most successful stories and essays. When you sit at your computer, hell-bent on coming up with some important concept, you are asking for trouble; before you know it, you will be jotting down big themes like "man's inhumanity to man," or intractable problems like the proliferation of motorized scooters on our city sidewalks. That's all fine if you're on the editorial staff of some newspaper, but for the rest of us, that kind of material is dead on arrival. Killed by noble intentions.

Meanwhile, the stuff you scorn, the quotidian chaff that your mind keeps turning over and over, is where your fortune lies. Let the big themes emerge, if they will, from the everyday questions, the *Sturm und Drang* of your daily existence, from the stuff with which you are, for good or ill, consumed. Pay attention to what's playing in your head at any old time of the day, and don't be so quick to dismiss it. You could be passing over your most fertile ground, the soil from which your best work might, with a little sunshine and water, one day grow.

RULE 6.

DON'T OVERINFLATE THE BALLOON.

Attuning your antenna to the mundane is also a good way to ward off another affliction. The problem is an insidious one, and its seeds are usually sown in high school when a teacher innocently asks "And what does the white whale really stand for?" or "Why does Holden Caulfield dream of being a catcher in a field? And why, specifically, a field of *rye*?"

The disease is called "symbolitis," and the further down that road you go, the more confused you and your writing will become.

When we study Literature—and I mean that with the capital L— we learn to comb over the text with a magnifying glass, looking for everything from religious iconography in Steinbeck to the metaphorical meaning of the paint factory in Ralph Ellison's *Invisible Man*. We're looking at everything *on* the page to see what else it might mean *off* the page. Is it by chance, or design, that a snake is seen in the swimming hole? Does the protagonist have the initials J.C.—as in Jesus Christ— for a reason? Does the scarlet letter have to be red? Before you know it, you start to think that that's how writers write—that they start out with some elaborate blueprint of mystical clues and meanings, which they cleverly embed and embroider in a narrative expressly designed and buttressed to carry the extra weight—when in fact they seldom do anything of the kind.

Writers write a story, not a theme. They write about things, not symbols, and characters, not icons. They write dialogue, not polemics. (At least the good ones do.) If symbols and themes emerge from the text, they only do so later on, and in most cases without the author even having been aware of them at the time he or she was writing. I know this is heresy in the eyes of the academic establishment, which sustains itself by foraging for such truffles, but if you ask me, much of what passes for literary analysis is about as reliable as astrology, and reveals a deep incomprehension of the creative act. If you were actually to set out with a symbolic and/or thematic edifice in mind, then you would have been better off becoming an architect than an author. A book is not an Erector Set.

And it isn't an enemy code, either, which you'd need the Enigma machine to decipher. Without getting too fundamentalist about it, it's the words, in black ink, on the white page. That's what you as a reader read, and that's what you as an author write. If you let things be what they are, and write about them faithfully and true, then you've done your job, and maybe, if you've done that job profoundly enough, you will have illuminated some greater truth or design. But deliberately trying to invest your work with meta-meanings is the surest route to madness; the more you inflate your writing, the sooner it will pop like a great big empty balloon.

RULE 7.

SKIP THE STARBUCKS.

For many writers, nothing goes better with a laptop than a double café mocha at the closest Starbuck's—and there are three of them on my street alone, not to mention half a dozen other such establishments, where almost every table is occupied by another earnest scribe.

The theory behind the Starbuck's School of Writing, to which countless aspiring writers subscribe, is simple—you'll do your best and most concentrated work when you're out of the house and losing yourself in a crowded café, surrounded by deafening cappuccino machines, swinging doors, and tiny tables jammed with equally striving strangers.

Of course, the theory is wrong—what you really get out of a trip to Starbucks is a nice caffeine buzz and the heady impression that you've been working when in fact you haven't.

Starbucks is where writers go who want to be *seen* in the act of creation, who treat writing as if it were some kind of performance art. They want to be admired, they want to be soothed by the ambient noise and the occasional glance from an attractive patron. They want to be asked, *What are you working on?*, so they can sit back and talk about it.

Or scowl importantly, and say, *Sorry, I can't be disturbed right now.*

When, if they really and truly wanted to be undisturbed, they'd stay home in the first place, make a cup of Folger's instant (for about a quarter), and concentrate.

I know the problem; I know the temptation. Nobody wants to lock himself up in a room and write. Neither do I. Most days I trudge into my office like a guy on a chain gang. It's lonely in there; I know I'll have no one to amuse me but me, and what if I can't come up with anything all that good? Sometimes, at a total loss, I just stare out the window at the guy in the apartment across the way; he's got a TV the size of a stadium jumbotron—and he likes to watch reruns of *The Office*, a show I enjoy. Lately, however, I've noticed, he's taken to lowering his blinds.

Still, it's in my own little office that the actual writing gets done.
In solitude.
In silence.
With no cappuccino machine anywhere in sight.
And no living witnesses to the act of creation.

When I do go to Starbucks—and I'm a sucker for those pump-kin-flavored drinks they serve in the fall—it's to reward myself for having done a good day's work. At home.

And instead of bringing my laptop, I carry the *New York Times Book Review*, so I can check out what the bestselling writers are up to and mutter dark conspiracy theories about how I've been unfairly overlooked.

RULE 8.

TAKE THE ZOLOFT.

Legend has it that once, long ago, in a land far far away, there was a writer who wasn't depressed.

But don't believe it.

Writing, in case you haven't yet noticed, can be a very depressing occupation. Not only do you have to sit in that room alone, brooding, you have to stop thinking about all your friends who are out there flirting among their cubicles at work, or hanging out at the old water cooler. (Say, it's been so long since I was even in an office, have water coolers gone the way of IBM Selectrics, once the apotheosis of writing machines?) If you weren't depressed when you started, trust me—you will be by the time you're done.

Now, a lot of people are under the impression that if they mess with their mood, they'll also mess with their art. Keats was depressed, Plath was depressed (to the point of suicide), Virginia Woolf was depressed (ditto), Hemingway was depressed (ditto again), William Styron was depressed (and wrote a very moving book about it, called *Darkness Visible*.) Bleakness of spirit is just the price you pay for artistic fulfillment and creativity. Right?

Wrong.

Depression can be crippling, making you unable even to sit at the keyboard or lift the pen, or it can be milder and chronic—what's called dysthymia—but either way, it's not helping your art, it's hurting it. It's sapping your confidence, disturbing your sleep, laying waste to your energy reserves. It's not the wellspring of your genius and creativity—it's the sump pump sucking your happiness and productivity down the drain. True, lots of writers, for time immemorial, have managed to work through it, but at what a terrible cost, to themselves and the people who have to sit down and share a kale smoothie with them in the morning. (Could that kale smoothie be part of the problem?)

Nor is depression all that picturesque. I know, it's easy to believe that you have to suffer for your art. Aren't creative types supposed to wear a lot of black and fly into a temper now and then? Aren't they duty-bound to be prickly and difficult? Not really. While it's a commonly held impression of the artistic temperament, I defy you to show me the manual that absolutely demands it.

So if you're in a bad way, take whatever antidepressant your medical professional may have prescribed. Or, and this is even simpler, just get out and see some friends. Catch a movie. Go to a ball game. Don't fear, as many writers do, that if you start having some fun and enjoying yourself, you'll somehow take away from your art. You won't. Your work will get better, you'll produce even more of it, and your loved ones won't be quite so sorely tempted to pack their bags and leave you in the dead of night.

RULE 9.

LOSE THE MUSE.

Of all the ways writers find to waste time, waiting for the muse to show up has to be the most common, and fruitless, of them all.

So if you're waiting for her, too, stop it right now.

The muse—the embodiment of inspiration, usually portrayed as a comely woman loosely draped in a diaphanous gown—is what every writer longs for. (But come to think of it, do women writers dream of hunky Highlander types in loose kilts instead? Just asking.) Once the muse, in whatever guise, does appear, you're supposed to be able to write effortlessly, at the height of your powers, with an unequalled command and energy and zest.

Must be nice.

As anyone who actually writes on a regular basis can attest, the muse is a very unreliable creature, sometimes showing up at noon, raring to go and sometimes at midnight just when you're ready to call it a day. And sometimes, no matter how many times you put out an SOS, your muse doesn't appear at all, return your calls, or come to your door (which you've left conveniently unlocked). Simply MIA. Gone without a trace. No forwarding address.

Which is why you cannot build your writing life around a muse's erratic schedule.

Sometimes, you'll feel inspired when you sit down to write—and sometimes you won't. That's just the way it is. But sit down you must, and write you will—and if there's one thing every writer learns over time, it's this: The muse is most effectively summoned by the clicking of your keyboard, or the scratching of your quill pen on parchment. Once you stop worrying about where the muse is, and focus instead on doing the work at hand, you're most likely to receive a visit. Most of the time, you'll be so absorbed in your work that you won't even notice when the muse has slipped into the room. You'll just keep on writing, your head down, your fingers flying, and only when you finish, and sit back with satisfaction to read over what you've done, will it dawn on you that you had company, after all. The evidence is all right there, on the pages in front of you.

The muse may come and go at will, silently and unseen, a phantom of unpredictable habits and mysterious ways. But there is one thing that every writer does get to know about this elusive entity over time— the aroma of hard work draws it like a bear to honey.

RULE 10.

GET ROLLING.

Getting started is, to my mind, the worst part of a writer's work. Every day it's like sitting down in a car that's been left outside in a snowstorm for three days and trying to get the engine to turn over. Press on the gas too gently and the car won't start, press on it too hard and you flood the engine. Not to mention chipping the ice off the windshield, so you can see where you're going. Yep, getting underway is a tricky business.

Which is why, for time immemorial, writers have been looking for ways to get around the problem. Ernest Hemingway made it a practice to stop writing somewhere in the middle of a passage that was barreling along really well. His theory was that he could then jump right into that section the next day, pick up the momentum where he'd left off, and keep right on rolling into the virgin territory beyond. The car engine, in his case, was always warm that way.

The English novelist Anthony Trollope was a meticulous craftsman, who had his daily quota, and stuck to it religiously. Every day he produced, I think it was, two thousand words, and if 1,950 of them completed the novel he was working on, then the following fifty were immediately applied to the next book he'd had in mind. For him, the car apparently started every time, without fail, so he hardly needed a method at all.

Philip Roth, according to an interview I once read, wrote a couple of pages a day, then spent the next day revising the last page or so, before plowing on from there. A slower way to start, for sure, but if it worked for Roth, who produced an impressive number of prize-winning books . . .

Personally, I've tried 'em all. Hemingway's approach is a good idea, but I found it very hard to make myself abandon work, to stop writing and walk away from a scene, just when things were rattling along. If the writing was really flowing, there was no way I was going to stanch or impede it in any way. The time or two that I did try stopping in midstream and returning the next day, it was never quite the same.

I always felt it would have been better if I'd simply let 'er rip the day before. Turns out, I'm no Hemingway.

One thing I do know, however—and that I highly recommend—is that you give some serious thought to where you will be plunging into your work the next time you sit down. Often, after finishing up a day's work, I've had some vague notion of where I'd start up again, but then I've made the fatal mistake of not jotting down any rudimentary notes or clues. I was so sure I'd remember it all the next day that I didn't think I had to. Well, I didn't remember, and you might not, either. And even if you do have some faint glimmering, you'll remain convinced that there's still something missing, that you had a much better, fuller, more intriguing, idea the previous day, and you'll then squander an hour kicking yourself for not being able to recall it.

Trust me, though—you didn't have a better idea. And the way to prove it, and avoid all the agonized second-guessing, is to start regularly making a few notes to yourself, as soon as you're done writing for the day. Leave yourself some indication as to where, to the best of your knowledge, the narrative is supposed to go next. Do it before you get up from your desk, do it before you turn out the light and go to sleep, but do it, one way or the other. That way you'll have *something* to look at the next morning, over the rim of your coffee cup, as you contemplate that frightful descent into the gaping maw of your manuscript.

RULE 11.

LET THE WELL REFILL.

Still, there will be times, long dark nights of the soul, when you don't know where your writing is going. When you're not sure what befalls your hero next, or you're unclear on how to develop your argument further, or you feel that your article is missing some important research element—but you're just not quite sure what it is.

And while sticking with it, staying on your work schedule, sitting down at your desk at the same time every day, is generally the best way to break the blockade, there are times, I will concede, when even that is not going to work.

At those times, take a break.

Henry James described it as letting "the well of unconscious cerebration" refill (but then, Henry James would put it that way, wouldn't he?). Still, the analogy is a good one. All your ideas come from deep inside you, from the well of what you think and feel and know and fear and love, and that well can occasionally become occluded, or it can seem to have gone dry (even though it hasn't really—and never will). But by focusing your energies elsewhere for a little while, you can give the well some time to replenish itself; this, for instance, would be a very good time to clean out the garage, reconnect with an old friend, or amortize the Peloton bike by removing the clothing from its handlebars and taking a vigorous ride.

It's also a matter of perspective. Sometimes you are simply so close to your work, so deeply enmeshed in its gears, that you can't see what's gumming things up. You have to step back, and step away, in order to see where the problem lies. It could be something as simple as a false plot turn, one that sent you careening off in the wrong direction, or it could be something as major as a loss of faith in the project (which I'll get to in greater detail shortly). Whatever it is, a short break can give you the time and the distance necessary to assess the difficulties, and ideally address them. Sometimes it's a quick fix, and sometimes— though you will shrink from it—the required repairs are extensive. If it's the latter, just roll up your sleeves and get to it. The longer you wait, or try to come up with some smaller, simpler way around whatever the problem is, the one that's staring you right in the face, the more time and energy you will ultimately waste.

The uglier the job, the better it is to tackle it head-on and straight-away. Why postpone the inevitable? Inevitable, as the word suggests, always wins.

RULE 12.

TELL, DON'T SHOW.

Wait—isn't that supposed to be the other way around, you may ask?
Not always.

Writers have been hearing about the importance of "showing" for so
long that they've begun to forget the value of "telling"—of exposition,
of summary, of omniscient narration.

If you've got something *worth* showing, then by all means show it. If
it's a dramatic action, let us see it happen. If it's a scintillating exchange
of dialogue, then let us hear it, every word. That should make up the
bulk of whatever you're writing.

But don't be afraid to *tell* us things, too. Don't be afraid to tell us,
with all your powers of description and even a bit of attitude, about an
atmosphere, a landscape, about what's going on in a character's mind,
or in the larger world of your story. Don't be afraid to enter into your
tale, to limn its greater dimensions and suggest its meanings. It was
good enough for Dickens, who told us right off the bat in *A Tale of
Two Cities*, that "It was the best of times, it was the worst of times," or
who opened *Bleak House* with an unforgettable description of the fog
descending on Chancery Court, the fog that would seem to envelope
and befuddle and frustrate all of the characters later to be drawn into
the unresolvable case of Jarndyce v. Jarndyce. Of course, leave it to
Dickens to pull off the neat trick of *telling* us something about what is
going to unfold in the book, something we don't yet know about, by
showing us something as common as a London fog. That, my friend, is
why he got the big bucks.

Don't think you have to show us the things we don't actually need
to see, either. If your heroine gets up in the morning and gets ready for
work, we don't need to see her take a shower, brush her teeth, make
coffee, butter her toast, and put on her shoes. We just need to know
she's on her way to work. Elmore Leonard, a master of pacing, once
said he keeps his books moving briskly along by leaving out all the
parts readers don't want to read.

The same goes for nonfiction. If you're writing a travel piece, you don't need to take us along every step of the way; you can jump straight from one port of call to the next. If it's a personality profile, feel free to give us a general impression of your interview subject; we don't need to hear every single word, or see every single action he or she performs. Use a fine brush when you have to, but take some broad strokes, too. Life is short, and so is the attention span of most magazine readers (a sadly diminishing population, as it is).

The omniscient voice, the one that knows everything and sees into the minds of all, is the voice that *tells*. But in so doing, it's the most intimate, the most powerful, and the most all-embracing voice imaginable. It's the voice you use, as an author, to whisper directly into your reader's ear, to offer a greater sense of your purpose, your design, and your own point of view. It's a chance to play God, and since those come along so seldom, it'd be a shame to pass up even one.

RULE 13.

PLAY GOD.

And while we're assuming the role of the deity, let's really go to town.

Anytime you confront the blank page, you're confronting a void, an emptiness, which you are about to fill. In so doing, you are about to bring into existence a whole new world—even if that world is going to be as small as a short story, or as large as *The Lord of the Rings*. Everything you put into it will be a part of that world, and everything you leave out will remain outside of it. Yes, we the readers, will bring to it all sorts of previously acquired knowledge, assumptions, information—Stephen Crane could assume we'd already heard of the Civil War before we sat down to read *The Red Badge of Courage*—but a well-wrought narrative establishes its own universe, in which we suspend, for the time being, what we already know, and accept the limitations and dimensions of the world we are about to enter.

We must also, however, be able to accept the rules and regulations of that world. We must find them credible and, above all, consistent. Does that mean you can't write a vampire novel in which the vampire gets around, untroubled, in the daylight? Or a movie like *Groundhog Day*, in which the hero keeps waking up and reliving the same day of his life, until he somehow manages to get things right? Of course not. You can create any wild, surreal, imaginary world you want, where white rabbits lead proper young ladies down holes in the ground, where budding wizards study sorcery in secret academies, where a magical ring holds unimaginable power, but whatever world you create, you are bound, as is your reader, by the logical parameters of that world. Whatever rules you set up—that dead people can be seen by one boy but no one else, that the monster will heed only his creator's commands, that the evil hotel needs to corrupt a human agent to feed its dreadful needs—you are restricted by those same rules, and if you break them, you do so at your peril. There's a bond of trust between you, the writer, and your readers. The reader is saying, "Take my hand, lead me anywhere you want, but I'm counting on you to keep me informed of how things work in this world." And you, in turn, are saying to your reader, "Come on along, don't sweat it, I'll show you the ropes. You may get a few surprises and scares along the way, but nothing that happens will break with anything that's been firmly established so far. If my vampire, who's been safely walking in the daylight in chapter one, suddenly explodes into flame at the touch of sunshine in chapter two, I'll at least account for it somehow." (Insufficient sunblock?) Once too many rules get broken, or even bent, the reader will begin to lose confidence in the story, and in its teller. After all, if anything can happen, at any time, for no particular reason, and following no particular logic, then nothing can really matter, ever. Who can blame the reader for losing interest?

RULE 14.

STOP READING.

Impossible, you may say. Writers read, all the time—and if they don't, they're not really writers.

I would not argue with that.

But I would say that once you've embarked on a writing project, the last thing you want to do is start filling your head with other people's prose, with their characters, their dialogue, with another writer's way of looking at things, or describing them.

What you're trying to preserve, what you're trying to protect, is your own voice, and your own approach. I remember that when I was in high school, and I had to write a paper on Herman Melville and *Moby-Dick*, I produced a paper that read like it had been written by a teenage Melville himself, filled with portentous prose, vague pronouncements, and syntax so elaborate that even I could not have unscrambled it. I was under the spell of a master, and I hadn't managed to shake myself out of it. (Still, I did get an A.)

Doing your own work now, you want to create your own spell, and that's hard enough to do without being under someone else's. In fact, the better the writer you might be reading, the more danger you're in. The style will be just that much more seductive, the work itself more compelling. You may settle down in your easy chair, convinced that reading just a few more chapters will do you no harm; you may even tell yourself that it will help you to make progress on your own work. But chances are, you'll keep on reading—reading is always so much easier than writing, and in almost every instance more fun—and before you know it, your own work may begin to shift, in its structure, its prose rhythm, its vocabulary, and even its ideas.

Reading bad stuff presents its own dangers. Although you're less likely to emulate or imitate it, you can still pick up some nasty habits, and your standards can start to fall, without your even noticing it. The cheap, brassy prose ceases to clang in your ear. The clichés start to seem permissible. (When I began to write articles for *New York Magazine*, I had to stop writing their subscription ads, which I'd also been doing; although I missed the extra income, I knew that writing junk like "Wow! That's a saving of 33 percent off the newsstand price!" was interfering with my higher calling.)

Still, you probably can't go cold turkey and stop reading altogether—I know, I've tried. But as a rule of thumb, try not to read anything too close to what you're working on, or that might in any way unduly influence you. In other words, when writing a sensitive novel, you might want to read only nonfiction, and even then only nonfiction that is well removed from your subject matter. For instance, if I'm writing fiction, that's when I read a big fat biography of someone long dead. Or else I just resort to newspapers and magazines. The deeper I am into a big project—novel, screenplay, opera libretto (just kidding about that last one)—the more I turn to periodicals to get my reading fix. You can read a few articles, finish them in one brief sitting, and toss the paper or magazine aside. Unless it's one of those pieces as absorbing as it is extensive, the kind that run in the *New Yorker* and almost nowhere else anymore, there's very little chance of your being taken away from your own work for too long, or too irresistibly. You'll be away just long enough to satisfy your craving for new and other words, and refreshed enough to throw yourself back, reinvigorated, into the creation of your own distinctive magnum opus.

RULE 15.

DON'T GET TRENDY.

I have a writer friend who spends more time trying to catch the next publishing wave than he does actually writing anything. So consumed is he with whether the horror market is up or down, the thriller market saturated, the romance shelves stocked or barren, that he seldom gets around to figuring out what it is he really wants to write himself. He's a publishing speculator more than he is an active participant. And his system—trying to writing sci-fi when that appears to be making a resurgence, or hacking out a dark domestic mystery when those seem to be popular—"The Girl on the Greyhound Bus!" "The Woman in the Carpool Lane!"—has been an utter bust.

Not that that keeps him from trying.

The thing about waves, in publishing and in popular taste, is that by the time you spot one, it's invariably too late to catch it. So don't even try. Given that it takes roughly nine months, at best, to get a finished book out into the marketplace (and that's not counting the time it would actually take to *write* and *sell* such a book in the first place), you can see that there's little point in trying to assess and extrapolate anything, with certainty, from the current situation. Right around the time you drag yourself, and your project, across the finish line, you will look up to see that everything has changed while you were hunkered down in your lonely bunker.

Not to mention the more critical problem, which is that nobody's good at everything. Henry James wanted to be a playwright, but that just wasn't his forte. (Of course, I know many people who, having struggled through *The Golden Bowl* in college, would claim that novels weren't either.) When you try to write the kind of material that you don't really respond to yourself—whether it's a black humor piece for a magazine, a disaster-flick screenplay, a coming-of-age novel— you've got to remember that you're up against a thousand other writers who really *do* like that particular kind of stuff, and who, as a result are bound to do it a lot better than you do. My father, God bless him, who was always worried about my prospects, kept advising me to stop doing what I was doing and write "one of those John Grisham novels," instead. No matter how many times I told him that if it was that easy, John Grisham wouldn't be John Grisham, he always believed I was just being stubborn.

And as for that vast theoretical marketplace, the one where one genre is going up and another one is going down, keep in mind that the good stuff always finds its way. Just because publishers may not be as interested in military hardware thrillers as they once were, it doesn't mean that they've lost interest altogether. And just because the Hollywood studios say they don't want to see sports-oriented scripts anymore doesn't mean the right one won't change their minds. (Before Sylvester Stallone wrote *Rocky*, which went on to win the Academy Award for Best Picture, boxing movies were anathema.) If it's done with enough conviction and style and narrative drive, there's a market out there for nearly anything. Write it right and you won't have to find your audience—they'll find *you*.

RULE 16.

WRITE WHAT
YOU READ.

Take a look at your bedside table and tell me what—besides the alarm clock, the TV remote, and the empty ice cream container from last night—is sitting there.

A book, perhaps?

If so, what kind of book? (And don't lie just to impress me.)

Is it a romance novel? A techno-thriller? A sword and sorcery epic?

Odds are, whatever kind of book is sitting on your bedside table—or is waiting for you on your Kindle or iPad—that is the kind of book you should be writing yourself.

Why?

Because, clearly, that's what you most enjoy. That's the kind of book you curl up with at the end of the day, or when you want to take a work break. It's what you read for pure pleasure.

And the kind of book you read for pure pleasure is the kind of book you will stand the best chance of writing well yourself.

Successful writing is writing done with conviction. It's writing in which the author was truly invested. If what you like is spy stories, that's fine; no reason to be ashamed, and even less reason to try to write the kind of mainstream literary novel (a deeply revealing portrait of middle-aged anomie in America's heartland, or whatever) that you would never voluntarily pick up yourself.

If you wouldn't read it, you will not be able to write it.

By writing the sort of thing you enjoy reading, you give yourself another advantage, too—especially when you're writing your first book or two. Instead of venturing into uncharted territory, you're treading familiar ground, where you instinctively know the terrain, the landmarks, the most successful routes to the ultimate destination. Even if you couldn't articulate these things, you know them in your bones, just from having been there so many times before—and when you write, you'll be aware, pretty soon, if you have veered from the path. You'll also know how to get back on it.

Every kind of writing has its own conventions, from the climactic love scene in a romance novel to the shoot-out in a Western. You know what you would expect from such a book, and so you know, too, what your readers will expect from yours. Put that knowledge and expertise to use. Write what you would want to find on your own bedside table, and there's a very good chance you'll have written something that lots of other people will want to put on theirs, too.

RULE 17.

MAKE 'EM WORRY.

If there's one thing you want your readers to do, it's worry.

Huh? Doesn't everyone hate to worry?

Not when it comes to reading. Worry is what keeps people turning the pages. Will your characters survive? Will they prevail? Will they overcome all the obstacles you throw in their way and, in the end, get what they want? Your mission is to keep your readers guessing.

Imagine if you wrote a story in which everybody started out knowing exactly what they wanted, and then in short order got it. What kind of story would that be? How would it get readers involved? Who would it leave them to root for? And how on earth would you manage to fill enough pages to make a story, much less a book, out of it?

No, the essence of any story is obstacles and, yes, you've heard this a million times before, *conflict*. The worst thing you can do for your characters is to give them an easy time of it. If they're meant to be lovers, make sure they're already engaged to other people. If your plucky heroine needs to make a fortune, make sure she loses one first. If she needs to get somewhere, make sure the road is washed out and there's an angry trucker on her tail. Your readers want to see, even savor, the struggle; they want to see the odds overcome, the hurdles jumped, the victories won. Imagine if Atticus Finch, the lawyer in *To Kill a Mockingbird*, had simply decided, given the bigotry of the townsfolk, that this case was unwinnable and refused to fight the charges against his innocent client.

Awfully short book, and we'd have missed out on a great movie, too.

Does that mean your story has to end happily?

Absolutely not. Just ask Madame Bovary or Anna Karenina.

Heck, even a good newspaper story makes us worry some. I just read a story in the local paper about a grave miscarriage of justice; a hung jury let some guilty people off the hook. (Plainly guilty, because the criminals had made a videotape of their crime.) I knew from the headline that it was a mistrial, but I read on to find out what had derailed the prosecution's case and to hear whether or not the malefactors would be retried, or escape unscathed. And then, another article, published in the same issue of the paper, got me worried about the massive pile of plastic debris floating in the ocean. What, apart from recycling my bottles and cans, I could do about the problem, was unclear, but I did feel like I at least had to worry about it for a while. So I did give it that.

In art, as in life, things don't always work out for the best. But in art, just as in life, what makes things interesting and memorable is how events play out. How do people play the hand that's dealt them? Do they fold, or do they bluff? Do they conserve what they have left, or do they raise the ante? It doesn't matter if you're writing a novel, a memoir, or an exposé—you want to keep your audience wondering how things will turn out, worried that they might not go well, and unable to stop reading until they've found out for themselves.

RULE 18.

MEMO YOURSELF.

Every writer has at least one of these—the great idea that got away. The brilliant story twist that came in a flash, and departed just as quickly. The beautiful turn of phrase that would have perfectly capped the epic poem. The stunning insight that would have finally yielded the unified field theory that eluded Albert Einstein.

All lost, for want of . . . what?

A pad? A pen? Okay, that's easy enough to remedy. Any writer worth his ink learns to carry something around with him to record his thoughts and inspirations. (Remember that journal, mentioned earlier, that I recommended you burn? If you didn't do that yet, you can use it for this instead.) Balzac made notes wherever he went, and *The Human Comedy*, all thirty-eight volumes of it, is stuffed with the material he relentlessly accumulated every day.

These days, of course, most of us have a cell phone on us except when we're in the shower. (Personally, I must have some secret aversion to it, since I seem to forget to carry mine a whole lot of the time. I never forget my wallet, my comb, my keys, even my Altoids, but that damn cell phone routinely slips my mind. I think I really don't want to be reachable much of the time.) Anyway, use your phone, then, to send yourself a text or email, or record a voicemail message to yourself (that you'll only have to transcribe to some more permanent file later on), but okay. Whatever works for you.

The larger problem, however, remains—training yourself to *do* it! I know, I know, you *think* you'll remember all the good ideas that cross your brainpan. An intriguing thought will come to you, and you'll smile and tuck it away in a mental file folder, which you'll then dutifully deposit in the "short-term memory" vault of your cerebral cortex.

Where, trust me, it will crumble to dust before you can ever find it again.

Even in a matter of hours, it will be gone. Look all you want, but all you'll remember is a fragment, a tantalizing piece of the amazing, and breathtakingly original, whole. And that taste—worse than forgetting the thing in its entirety—will torment you like a bad commercial jingle you can't get out of your head.

How much better would it have been to have simply jotted down a note or two at the time you first had this breathtaking idea?

My mother, a writer herself, always slept with a pad and pen on her bedside table, and once, in the dead of night, she had a dream of the perfect locked-room mystery story. A man found murdered, alone, in a third-floor study, locked from the inside. The only window firmly closed, with no rope hanging from its sill or footprints in the soil below. No balcony, no fire escape. When she woke up and remembered scrawling down the solution to the mystery, she grabbed the pad, and eagerly read some notes, in her sleepy handwriting. Their headline read, "The tree outside the window did it!"

Upon reading the rest, or what she could make out of them, it turned out that, although the tree's motive remained unresolved, it had slipped its branches through the window, strangled the victim in his sleep, then quietly closed the window again after withdrawing.

Another arboreal murder.

So okay, maybe everything you jot down isn't worth preserving. But for every killer tree idea, you'll find a dozen ideas that *are* still good, even in the cold hard light of day. They may need a little more nurturing to come into their own, but at least you've got the seeds to work with.

RULE 19.

TAKE LIBERTIES.

If you're writing an article about world trade regulations, it's essential you get all your facts and all your statistics exactly right.

If you're writing a profile of a movie star or politician, it's critical that you record your quotes accurately.

If you're writing a history of warfare at sea, it's important that you know everything possible about clipper ships and aircraft carriers, sextants and sonar, torpedoes and Trafalgar, etc.

But, and this is a big but, if you're writing an imaginative work, something clearly billed as fictional, your responsibilities are a bit different—to both the reader and yourself.

First of all, you don't have to make yourself quite as crazy when it comes to the research. Oh sure, if you want to make sure every single thing is scrupulously accurate and well-documented, go right ahead. You can easily devote months, even years, to doing all the necessary research, to combing through library stacks, dusty archives, and dense websites. You can prepare the factual ground for your work of fiction for as long as you like . . . but there's a good chance (I've seen it happen) that by the time you near the end of your research, you will also have lost the impulse that made you embark on it in the first place. You'll have gone beyond what was really necessary and lost yourself in the morass of detail.

In creating a work of fiction, you're asking the reader (or viewer, if it's a screenplay) to accept your take on the world—the world, that is, you've specially constructed for the purposes of your story. If you've done your job right, your audience is convinced of that world's plausibility and they're willing to go along for the ride. You don't want to do anything that will jar them out of that world—introducing, say, a rifle in ancient Rome, or a buccaneer who claims to be "stressed out" by his occupation.

But that doesn't mean you have to have unassailable facts to back up every single thing in your narrative. In other words, if you're writing a story about an art dealer in old Amsterdam, you can make up a secret canal or two. If you're writing a story about the CIA, you can imagine yourself, and your reader, into an inner sanctum of your own design. (The chances of your getting an invitation to the real one are small.) If you're writing a sci-fi adventure, you may even have to alter, or make up, some of the rules of travel in the space-time continuum. In one novel I wrote, I included some complex brain physiology, and I did hear from an old, high school friend who'd gone on to become a brain surgeon: "You might want to give me a call," he advised, "the next time you're describing a brain dissection." Apparently, I'd placed a pesky little gland or two in the wrong spot. Picky, picky . . .

Although he was undoubtedly correct, my other readers were never bothered. And so long as none of them trusted my novel to tell them how to do brain surgery, I was unperturbed. I felt I had done my job if I'd been able to carry them through that part of the story with enough verisimilitude that they didn't doubt my credibility, or lose confidence in the world I had drawn them into. In fiction, veracity is nice, laudable, lovely—more power to you—but believability is all that you're really required to provide and all that your audience has a reasonable right to expect.

RULE 20.

KNOW THE TERRITORY.

In a close corollary to the rule above, there's one other thing to consider when creating your fictional world.

How ordinary and familiar would that world be to a general audience? Because it makes a big difference.

I could get away with making a mistake in describing a brain surgery (almost), but if I tried to describe a visit to the supermarket, where I spotted several movie stars pushing their own carts, I'd be pushing my luck. Readers have shopped at supermarkets themselves, they know you seldom see celebrities there, and they know it's a pretty mundane experience all in all. Unless I can somehow account for those celebs— I'm shopping in Beverly Hills? Plus there's a citywide strike of household staff?—I've violated reality to such an extent that nothing else I write is going to seem credible. I have ventured, whether I planned to do so or not, into the surreal.

An aspiring novelist once submitted to me a romance novel about a secretary who worked in Manhattan. The secretary drove a Porsche, spoke several languages, and parked her car in the company lot before taking it out again to drive to lunch. I could get past the trilingual secretary, with the expensive sports car, but I somehow couldn't get past the company parking lot in the middle of Manhattan or the part about driving to lunch. I lived in New York, and I knew that that just wasn't the way life is lived there. People—secretaries especially—took the subway to work, and for lunch they walked around the corner to the deli. The sheer pileup of unlikely details finally did me in, and I couldn't accept much else that followed in the book.

The better the locale is known—and New York, for instance, *is* known, through TV and books and movies, pretty much to everyone— the closer you have to adhere to its actuality. (In one novel I wrote, set in Manhattan, I placed the make-up counters in Bloomingdale's on the wrong side of the store, and I got three complaints from readers about it!) The same rule holds true when you're writing about a few other spots—San Francisco better not be flat, Seattle shouldn't be arid. If you're not familiar with these places, and don't want to check your details, make up a city of your own, or place the action in a town less well-recognized.

Follow the same precept when it comes to what happens. The more an experience is familiar to people—shopping at the supermarket, going to the dentist, washing the car—the more you have to stay true to it. Everyone knows how those go, and to alter them too much—unless you're doing it deliberately, for a reason—is to risk inducing in your readers an unwelcome crisis of faith.

RULE 21.

SETTLE DOWN.

All writing is set somewhere.

In most nonfiction, the setting is determined for you. If you're writing a magazine profile of a reclusive heiress, you are going to need to describe the ten-foot-high hedge that conceals her unmarked estate, the long winding drive that leads to the ivy-covered Tudor manse, the bibelot-cluttered rooms. And you would be crazy *not* to linger on these things. They not only tell us about *how* she lives, they also tell us *who* she is. Setting, in this respect, *is* character.

In fiction, you even get to *choose* the setting. (How lucky can you get?) Your characters are going to live exactly where you tell them to live. In a fishing port on the Gulf Coast? So be it. Among the vineyards of Sonoma County? Okay. Your choice of locale is, of course, going to determine a great deal of what is to follow—it's going to be hard to write a convincing rodeo scene set in Philadelphia—but it's also going to color in your characters. If your heroine lives in Beverly Hills, then we might jump to the conclusion that she's rich and privileged, like those (so-called) Real Housewives on Bravo TV. But maybe she's not. Maybe she's living there on a shoestring, in a run-down garden apartment, among people she despises for the affluence and ease of their own lives. (Trust me—I know women on both sides of that particular fence, and boy, do they have stories to tell.)

That's why it's so critical that you address your setting in two ways: first, as you and your readers might perceive it, and second, as your character does. If your hero's living in the suburbs, is it by choice, or because it's where his wife and kids dragged him kicking and screaming all the way? It doesn't matter which you choose; what matters is that we feel the character is grounded, that he truly exists in a time and a place, and that we know how he feels about it. By positioning your character in a specific spot, you get to show him to us in either agreement with, or in opposition to, the place. If, for instance, he feels marooned in the suburbs, he can rail about the boring barbecues and the identical green lawns. If he loves it, he can sing the praises of out-door cooking and meticulous landscaping.

As an added benefit, the place, too, begins to assume character and dimension, so that every time your hero sets foot on the train platform or the freshly mown grass, we not only know what he's thinking, we feel the impact of the surroundings ourselves. Bucolic, suburban para-dise, or sterile, green hell—it could go either way, but it's going to add a lot to the picture no matter what. (Personally, I'm a city guy, except for the nights a car alarm goes off, and then I pine for the quiet of the burbs.)

RULE 22.

PICK YOUR POISON.

Of the thousand and one reasons not to write—and trust me, I know 'em all—the one that lies at the base of most of them is fear. Fear of failure, fear of success (I've heard of this one, but I'm still not sure I believe it), fear of confronting whatever personal demons and issues your writing may elect to address. Do you tell it like it is, or do you sugarcoat the truth? Do you keep your aspirations small—letters to the editor, fillers for the local paper, blog items—or do you kick out the jams and embark on a major opus? Do you stop complaining about trying to work at the kitchen table, surrounded by family commotion, and instead take the bold step of renting a small office somewhere?

For all its rewards, spiritual and otherwise, writing is a scary business. I wouldn't lie to you. You're facing more than the blank page, or screen, every time you sit down to work—you're facing a silent challenge, even a reproach. *Go ahead*, that white page says, *give me your best shot—throw some words at me and let me show you just what I think of them! I've faced down bigger opponents than you, and I ain't scared.*

Whether you like it or not, you have now entered what is commonly called a no-win situation. If you give in to your fears, and let the blank page remain unsullied, you will have simply traded one negative feeling—fear—for another one—regret. You'll not only feel bad about yourself, for cowardice in the face of composition, but you'll always wonder what you might have been able to accomplish if you'd just forced yourself to blunder on ahead. Every time you go into a bookstore, you'll be looking at the new titles with a hint of envy in your eye, wondering how your own book might have stacked up to all these others, and what it might have looked like—would it, too, have had a glossy cover, all bold type and vibrant colors, or would it have been something more discreet and tasteful? Even worse, one day you'll find on the shelf some book that reminds you of the one you were planning to write and *it just won't be as good as yours would have been.* That's a real killer. You want to yell at the top of your lungs, "Hold on! I had this idea first! And my book would have been even better!"

But of course you won't holler (not least of all because the security guard would throw you out of the store) but because it's too late—you had your chance and you didn't take it. That taste of ashes in your mouth is regret, and it's something all the mints in the world can't get rid of. But fear, on the other hand . . . why, that evaporates with every word you write. Just do your work, and—mirabile dictu!—the fear dissipates altogether, and the regret, of course, never has the chance to materialize. With any luck, the only thing you'll be left to contend with at the end of the day is that so-called fear of success. (Please write and tell me what that's all about. I still don't get it.)

RULE 23.

SHUT OUT THE NOISE.

Sometimes, the one thing keeping you from writing is the noise.

No, I don't mean the thumping bass of a neighbor's stereo, the sirens from the street, or the lawn mower next door. You can be writing in a mountain cabin, at the end of a dirt road, where there's no electricity and not a soul for miles around, and still find the noise deafening.

The noise, that is, inside your own head.

There are voices in there, and they're not necessarily your friends. They're harsh and critical and controlling. They say things like, "That idea isn't so original," or "Is that the best you can do?" or "What makes you think you're a writer? You're an accountant, for goodness sake!" It's like carrying around your own internal Greek chorus of naysayers . . . and they never shut up.

But you've got to make them.

Nobody writes without his or her critical apparatus up and func-tioning. You do need that voice that occasionally whispers in your ear, "Let's find a better word for that," or "Wouldn't it be nice to insert an authoritative quote right here?" It's called *thinking*. But you can't let that voice get out of hand and overwhelm you, slow you down or, as can happen, bring you to a grinding halt.

There isn't a writer alive who doesn't have to go back to do some fix-ing, tweaking, revising. Writing is rewriting, that's a common axiom. But right now, if you hit a snag and you can't seem to get through it, just go *around*. I will sometimes type, in all caps, gibberish where I know something, or some section, needs to be gone back to. Or I'll throw in the initials TK, which stand, improbably enough, in pub-lishing circles, for "to come." If it's an article I'm writing, it might be because I know I'm going to have to do some more research before filling in that portion, but with a deadline looming (deadlines always help in this respect), I'll just skip ahead to a place where I *do* know the terrain and start writing there. (I don't *like* doing things that way—I

like writing things in a straight line—but sometimes you don't have
the luxury of that option.)

It's that perfectionist voice that does the most damage, the one that
keeps kvetching about everything you do, that keeps telling you your
stuff isn't good enough, that you should start over, that you shouldn't
write the third sentence until the first two are pristine. Until you can
quiet down that voice, and make a temporary truce with it, you will
never get anywhere. You've got to make peace with yourself, some sort
of pact that says, "You know what? I'm going to write as well as I can,
and that's all I can do. And then, once I've got something down, I'm
going to go back and see if I can make it better." If you have to, promise
your inner perfectionist that you'll never send anything out without
giving it a thorough once-over, that you'll pay for a copy editor out of
your own pocket if need be, that you'll tithe ten percent of your writing income to a fund for dangling participles. Make any deal you have
to . . . but shut down that carping voice in your head long enough to
allow you to hear yourself think.

RULE 24.

MAP THAT ROUTE.

Of all the words that bring dread to the heart of a writer, perhaps none does the trick better than "outline." Even typing it now makes my heart clench in my chest, my eyes glaze over, my thoughts flee. For me, the very word conjures up images of my eighth-grade classroom, with Mrs. Hughes standing at the blackboard leading a drill, explaining that for every I there must be a II, for every *a* there must be a *b*, and so on. Whenever outlining is called for, I feel an irresistible impulse to run for the hills.

And yet, I have seen the best minds of my generation tear out their hair and give up on some of their most promising efforts, all for *want* of an outline. I have seen friends rip into a screenplay, only to collapse in confusion in the middle of the second act. I have seen novelist buddies stumble to a halt midway through their tale, the various threads of their narrative hanging between their fingers like tangled strings of Christmas-tree lights. I have read drafts of my friends' articles that circled back on themselves, that sprawled listlessly over page after page, and that had to stop, periodically, to remind the reader (and the writer) what the piece was about and what point it was trying to make. And though some of these mistakes would have emerged anyway—no one's first draft comes out perfect—outlining would have allowed the writer to avoid many of them.

But what do we mean by an outline? First let's get that straight. It doesn't have to be anything as formal as the diagrams Mrs. Hughes made us do. But it does have to be a plan—a serviceable road map that lays out most of the terrain ahead, the natural landmarks, the big scenes, the boffo conclusion. Obviously, an outline for a book or a movie script will have to be longer and more complete than one you would do for an article, but whatever the project, it will help you inestimably to have spent time, before you start writing, just sitting in a chair scrawling down all the things that you plan to include in the piece. Some people use index cards, some have the luxury of corkboards or blackboards where they work. Some do what's called a "cluster" outline, simply by writing down the topic—"Halloween in the Heartland," say—in the center of a page, then writing all around it the various things that the topic suggests. "Trick or treat," "popcorn balls and candy corn," "costumes," "pumpkin-carving," "bonfires." Then, it's just a matter of connecting these parts to each other and mustering them into some sort of order using squiggly lines and numbers and arrows.

Plan your journey any way you want—with elaborate schematics, or weird idea trees, or cryptic notes that even da Vinci could not crack—but do plan it. (If you want to make Mrs. Hughes happy, you can even do it in the rigorous, old-fashioned way.) For every half hour spent planning, you'll save countless hours, maybe even days, later on. But don't twist yourself into knots over it. Remember, you're not creating the fully-fleshed-out body of the piece—you're just trying to create a rickety coat rack that will stand up long enough for you to hang the clothes on it later.

RULE 25.

WING IT.

And now, now that I've convinced you to make your plan, be prepared to scuttle it.

The outline hasn't been written that a writer ever stuck to—not all the way, at least.

The outline, or whatever other plan you might have drawn up, is just one way you could have completed your assignment; it's one way that would have allowed you to cover all your material, or tell your whole story, from start to finish, without too many detours or digressions.

But it was never the *only* way.

The beauty of writing, of any creative endeavor for that matter, is in the discovery, and that part comes chiefly with the doing of it. It's only as you write that your thoughts completely coalesce, that your argument takes on its most persuasive form, that your characters come alive, that your story suddenly swerves in unexpected directions. It's only in the writing, I find, that you fully wake up. It's only in the process of writing, in fact, that you truly discover what it is you *think*.

But that doesn't make your plan or outline any less useful—your plan simply becomes, shall we say, malleable. Alter it as much as you like. Make it conform to what you're writing, and use it to look ahead and see what possible problems might now have been created down the line. Did you just give away a plot point that must, for other reasons, remain a mystery? Did you just kill off a character you're going to need later on? Have you stumbled onto a subplot, one that had never occurred to you when writing the outline, but that you now find neatly resonates with your main story? (That's a great feeling, when it happens. A tribute, I always feel, to the subconscious mind.)

If it's nonfiction, ask yourself if you've established all the things you needed to establish, and in the right order. Say you're writing about the physicists' latest plaything, super-string theory (better you than me, pal). Have you sketched in enough of the Newtonian, then Einsteinian, then quantum theory, to make your argument for seven dimensions immediately clear to even a lay reader? (Personally, I have enough trouble navigating in just the three we've got.)

Your outline is a crutch, there when you need it, and a solace when, in the dead of night, you think you'll never be able to figure out how to finish this project. The outline tells you it *can* be done, that, if all else fails, there's a working plan you can fall back on. But when you find yourself running ahead of it, when you see things unfolding naturally, organically, spontaneously and right before your eyes, forget about the planned itinerary. Don't let any outline or diagram slow you up for even a minute. Just keep on running—you're in the flow state—and only take a break when you run out of breath, inspiration, or paper.

RULE 26.

DON'T LOOK BACK.

As my mother used to say, "A job worth doing isn't necessarily a job worth doing well." This went for making beds, ironing pajamas, sweeping the back porch. It was enough, in her view, that it was done at all—it was pointless to put more time into it than the job warranted.

The same holds true, in my book, for first drafts. Because that's what they are—first drafts. Amateur writers hate to hear about drafts, because they believe, truth be told, that once they've written something, it's done. They can hardly wait for the page to come out of the printer so they can get it into the mail and off to the publisher.

But real writers—writers who get published—know better. They know that a first draft is going to be a *working* draft, a first run-through for the finished product, full of accidental tangents and infelicities of style. But that doesn't stop them from turning one out—and more importantly, it doesn't stop them from getting all the way from the start to the finish, from "Once upon a time" to "and they lived happily ever after."

That sounds easier than it is—and one reason many writers never get to the finish line of their first draft is because they keep looking back; they keep trying to fix every little thing on page ten before they move on to page eleven. For most of us, that is a formula for disaster—and incompletion. You will never get every word exactly right (I still cringe at certain passages when I read my old books). But if you plow ahead, if you make sure that every day you move your book or article or script just a *little bit* forward, eventually you will get to the end. Eventually, you will have a complete—however sloppy and prolix—manuscript. And that's when the real work begins—cutting, shaping, smoothing, and emending. In some cases, you will even want to go back and make wholesale changes—bolstering one character, eliminating another, dropping an entire section that no longer feels as essential as it once did. (Does your think piece about hip-hop really need that long digression about the twelve-tone scale?) Whatever. But the only way to get to this polishing stage—to the second, or third, or fourth draft—is by completing the all-important first draft. And the only way to complete that first draft is to damn the torpedoes and go full speed ahead. Don't worry about the imperfect prose you may have left behind in your wake; you can—and you will—circle back again later and clean things up.

RULE 27.

LET IT MARINATE.

If there's anything better than the feeling of satisfaction you get from completing a piece of work, it's the thrill you get from slapping it into an envelope and mailing it off into the world, or hitting SEND on the completed file. For days, weeks, even months thereafter, you can go to bed at night dreaming of the call you'll get from an editor, or the urgent text from an agent, the deals you will be offered, the extravagant sums that will be bandied about. (Is it too soon, you wonder, to start looking into a numbered Swiss bank account?)

But delightful as these fantasies are (and some may, indeed, come true), the one thing that might stand in your way is impatience. You may, out of an understandable eagerness to see your work in print, let it go out the door before it is really ready. You've prepared for this race a long time—so it's absolutely critical that you do not jump the gun now.

No matter how long you've worked on the project, no matter how many drafts you've gone through, it's a very good idea to wait—just a little—before actually submitting it anywhere. With an article or essay, it means holding on to it for a day or two, at least. (With an op-ed, keyed to some recent newsworthy event, however, you may not be afforded that luxury.) With a longer work, it might mean a couple of weeks. And that means not working on it—not even *reading* it— during that time. It *especially* means not reading it. Just let the work marinate, as it were, in your desk drawer or your computer file, and then, after enough time has passed that you can read it over with a passably fresh eye, do so.

You'll be amazed at what you find there.

You'll find sentences that bump along awkwardly, paragraphs that don't belong, bon mots that no longer seem so *bon*, typos, and misspellings. You'll wonder how you could have missed these things, but the answer to that one is easy: You were too close to the work. You knew every nuance of the prose, every beat, every twist and turn and transition. It's not that you couldn't see the forest for the trees; you couldn't see the trees for the twigs. What you needed was some distance, some perspective, and most of all, you needed to get the rhythms of your own work sufficiently out of your head to allow you to encounter the work as strangers would, as your audience will. They don't *know* what's coming, they don't *know* where you're going. And now, when you read it over, ask yourself if *you* do. Are there spots where even you, the author, had to pause for a moment to get your bearings? (An editor just questioned a brief passage in the manuscript of my novel in progress, and when I read it over, even I couldn't figure out what I'd been trying to say there!) It happens to every writer now and then. But the good ones know that by holding on to the work for just that little extra bit, by giving it a final once-over in the cold light of a new day, or the next week, they stand a much better chance of eventually seeing it in print.

RULE 28.

OVERCOME YOUR SEPARATION ANXIETY.

Of course, for every writer who sends his work out into the world too soon, there's another who hangs on to it for too long. My old pal Charlene was a professional writer, but getting her to part with her work was harder than getting Pharaoh to release the Israelites. Until her editors called, cajoled, and finally threatened legal action, she would not let the manuscript out of her hands.

Why is this? Why do writers hate to let go? Oh, I can think of several reasons, ranging from perfectionism to fear of rejection, but whatever is holding you back, there comes a time when the work has just got to leave the premises. You've done your best, you've let it marinate, you've made any and all final corrections—it's time now to send it into the public arena. The rest is up to Fate.

Not sending the work out within an acceptable time-frame is self-destructive in many ways. If what you've been writing is an article, or even an essay, there's a good chance that something in it is timely, that the idea occurred to you because of something in the news, something you recently read, something you've noticed around you. Well, believe it or not, other writers out there may have taken notice, too. I can't tell you the number of times that students in my classes have shown me work that they thought was absolutely original and startling, only to discover that someone else, in the very same class, had already written on the same topic. There is a zeitgeist, a spirit of the age that surrounds all of us, all the time, and we all tap into it for our ideas. In Hollywood, it's common knowledge that, unbeknownst to each other, several screenwriters are simultaneously working on scripts based on almost identical premises. It happens all the time. (Once, when I was reading scripts for a movie studio, I came across half a dozen screenplays in one month about tornado-chasers.) Ideas are wafting in the air all around us, like so many butterflies, and working writers never leave home without their nets.

Too much delay can be fatal in another way, too. The longer the manuscript sits on your desk, unread, unsubmitted, unchallenged, the more stale and uninspired it will begin to appear in your own eyes, too. It's like something you once loved—that spiffy new overcoat, that painting you acquired to mount above the fireplace, your new sweetheart—which, with time, has lost its luster and allure. You stop noticing it, you stop holding it in such high regard—you start wondering, in fact, what you ever saw in it in the first place. You may be tempted to start tinkering, a process that, once begun, seldom ends happily. It's an all-too-common impulse, but before you give in to it, drop the manuscript in the mailbox where you can't get at it again without committing a federal offense, or dispatch it electronically into the great ether from which nothing can ever be ineradicably rescinded.

RULE 29.

CALL "ACTION!"

The thing about creating a fictional world is, sometimes it just stops turning. The action grinds to a halt, the characters stop talking to each other, nothing happens next. You sit back and no matter how long you stare at the screen or the legal pad, nothing seems to break the stalemate.

At times like that, it might pay to sprinkle a little movie dust on your own eyelids. Here's how: Lean back in your chair, close your eyes, and pretend that the story or novel or script you're working on (this works especially well for scripts) is up there on the screen and you're just a passive audience member, munching your popcorn and watching it. Roll back the action a few minutes, watch as the characters go through their paces and the action unfolds, and then, when it gets to the part where you're stuck, just try to keep the movie running. Let the scene go wherever it wants to, or let it change altogether if that's what happens. Try not to interfere. Let it surprise you. Does somebody suddenly jump out a window? Do a couple of the characters get into a shouting match? Does the scene abruptly halt, only to be followed by a drastically different one—is the wild rave in an empty warehouse followed by a hushed conference in a library? Does the tender love scene turn into a jealous fight? Does the pitched battle give way to a sorrowful morning-after survey of the carnage?

By letting your mind run free, and the movie in your mind unspool, you're not only trying out different alternatives—various ways that the story can now move forward—but you're also, I believe, responding to something that has gotten you stuck in the first place. You weren't sure where to go next because you sensed your story needed a change—of pace, of tone, of setting. Something to shake it up and give it a jolt of whatever it had been lacking in the previous pages. If those pages featured small quiet scenes, then maybe what it needed now was something bigger, a scene at the county fair or a bit of derring-do. If all it's *been* is derring-do, maybe it needed a passage with less suspense

and more emotion. The movie in your mind is a good way of figuring that out. We're all so accustomed now to film techniques—pacing,
cutting, split screens, slow motion, flashbacks, flash-forwards—that
turning your story into a mental movie is a lot easier than you'd think.
We are all amateur directors! And putting yourself in the seat of an
eager moviegoer—rather than a stymied author—gives you a chance
to imagine, freely, filmically, what your story truly needs if you ever
expect it to clean up at the box office or the bookstore.

RULE 30.

PILE IT ON.

When it comes to writing, there is perhaps no more vilified part of the language than adverbs. Even Stephen King in his book *On Writing*, declares "the adverb is not your friend." (I almost wrote that he *flatly* declares it, but that would be using one of the adverbs he so detests.) Like many writers, he considers them weak and weaselly, words that cling to other words—verbs and even other adverbs—draining them of impact or just cluttering up the page. To King, an adverb is a "pernicious dandelion" to be rooted out the first chance you get.

Whew—I get it already, Steve.

But I'm still not ready to concede the point entirely.

While adjectives modify nouns and pronouns—an *athletic* girl, a *wounded soldier*, a *noble* stallion—adverbs give us the chance to modify verbs, usually with one of those words that end in "ly"—an athletic girl strode *confidently* into the arena, a wounded soldier ran *wildly* from the battlefield, a noble stallion rose up *defiantly*.

What drives most opponents of the adverb up the wall is the fact that these adverbs are being used—in their heated opinion—to do the work that a properly chosen verb, for instance, could and should have done on its own. For instance, instead of saying the soldier ran wildly, why not just say he charged? Instead of saying the stallion rose up defiantly, why not say it reared up? Isn't that easier and more to the point? Well, yes and no. In a lot of cases, it's true that the right verb can do the work on its own—and I, too, beseech you to search for the right one—but sometimes it can't. And I would submit that adverbs offer a lot of leeway and variety that we wouldn't otherwise have.

Take that stallion rearing up, for example—couldn't he have reared up anxiously, out of fear? And wouldn't that have been misunderstood, if the "defiantly" had not been thrown in for additional clarification? In the hands of a better writer, maybe it would have been entirely clear why the horse was rearing up—maybe we would know from the previous pages that this was one brave, unruly stallion—but then again, maybe not.

Adverbs get used in many instances, like the one above, for emphasis. The writer isn't sure he's made his case clearly enough, so he throws in what amounts to another stage direction, just to assure himself that his reader is getting the right picture. Maybe it makes the writer look overly eager to please, like a suitor showing up at the door with flowers, chocolates, *and* a corsage, but you can't blame the poor guy for trying; he just wants to make the right impression, and there's something kind of endearing, if a bit clumsy, about the attempt. If that's the worst writing crime you commit, throwing in some adverbs, you shouldn't be sentenced to anything more than a petty fine. (Unless, of course, Stephen King is the sitting magistrate. In that case, plead for your life.)

RULE 31.

REDUCE CLUTTER.

While we're talking modifiers, I can't resist my favorite, which appears often in the Los Angeles real estate ads. Along with all the dubious, over-the-top tributes to the property for sale, some ads proclaim that this is "an *emotional* house." The first time I saw it, I thought it was a misprint. But it's not. Although I can guess what the realtors, never known for their precise prose, are trying to say—that the house is so special it will *evoke* an emotional response in you—that's *not* what the ad as written is saying. Right now it's implying that the house has needs, feelings, and attitudes of its own—and I, for one, would not regard that as a selling point. What, you come home after a long day at the office and *your house* is in a bad mood? Your *house* needs you to make it a vodka tonic and listen to it rant about the awful day it's had?

Adjectives, which should be one of a writer's best friends, can misfire. See above. They can be misused, attached so that they suggest something not quite possible, or, more commonly, they can be scattered all over the page like confetti, where, instead of adding color to the prose, they obliterate it. This adjectival overload, the most prevalent form of abuse, I place at the door of creative writing classes. Virtually every creative writing teacher I had, from grade school through high school, encouraged drenching the story at hand in a thick syrup of goo. It was never a winter morning; it was always a "cold winter morning." It was never just a country inn; it was a "cozy country inn." No noun went into the world unmolested or unadorned.

And adjectives, like gang members, seldom ventured out alone. They went out in twos and threes, and God help us fours, and piled up on any person, place or thing that got in their way. "Look! It's a noun—let's get it!" For the reader, it became a bruising experience, as he or she tried to slog through the narrative without dropping from fatigue. When adjectives come, consistently, in pairs, or trios, or quartets—"The old red coach creaked down the long, winding, cobblestoned road and stopped before the timbered, mullioned, ancient tavern"—the hapless, weary, encumbered reader goes stark raving mad.

Adjectives are like spices that you throw into the stew; if they're helping, throw 'em in . . . judiciously. But the minute you sample the stew and it is overwhelmingly the spices, and not the stock, that you're tasting, stop. A little goes a long way.

RULE 32.

OFFER AN APPETIZER.

And while we're picking on adverbs and adjectives, why not take a moment to address the use of prologues in books? A lot of prominent writers like the late Elmore Leonard hate 'em. John Grisham is another. Even my friend and fellow novelist, Dave Fuller, thinks I should drop them from my books. "Why don't you just call them chapter one?" he says.

Which did give me pause.

But then I thought about it. My novels, at least the most recent batch, are historical suspense, and I use the prologue, rather than a simple first chapter, for a couple of reasons. You might, too.

For one, it sounds important. And I'm a sucker for cheap effects.

For another, the prologue is a way of starting the book with something exciting and even mysterious, a scene that grabs the readers by the lapels. It's like a teaser, offering a taste of something like the supernatural, the erotic, the nefarious, some element that will be borne out in the rest of the book to come. Think of it as an appetizer, or an amuse-bouche, a way of hooking the reader and leaving him or her wondering how this brief scene—and a prologue should never run more than a few pages—will tie into the action that begins with chapter one. I don't mind if that little question, hovering elusively overhead, takes a while to clear up.

Prologues are also generally removed from the time and place where the main action of the book begins. In my most recent novel, the one I've been working on for months, for example, the prologue takes place on the Western Front in World War I, while the first chapter of the book whisks us off to a period months later, in the English countryside, with characters not yet introduced, but who will now carry the story forward. We will return, of course, to that first dramatic scene, in due time, and address all the strange questions it raised, but for now, I'm content to let it rest. I just have to make sure that I do connect it to the rest of the story before the reader forgets all about it.

Once that's done, once you've gotten your own readers safely on board your own story, they will, one hopes, sail all the way to the last chapter with you. And that last chapter may well be an epilogue—a short chapter that is usually separated from the climax and the denouement of the book by some time and space; it can be used, as I do, to wrap up any last unresolved issues or plot points that are still dangling loose, or simply to ensure that your readers leave the book in the right frame of mind. I think an epilogue also makes for a classy bookend, suggesting that you were operating from some carefully wrought master plan, when in fact the book might have been cobbled together on the fly, with no idea of where it was going or how it would get there.

If the prologue stands just outside the front gate of the narrative, beckoning you to enter, the epilogue does a related service, waiting just behind the back gate to thank you for coming and politely usher you off the grounds.

RULE 33.

DON'T TENSE UP.

Even if Aristotle hadn't told us so, by now we'd have figured out that stories need a beginning, a middle, and an end. And the very fact that they do means that they're going to need a tense—a temporal frame in which the sequence of events unfolds. (E. M. Forster's formula of "and then . . . and then . . . and then . . .")

Generally, that's going to mean you'll be writing your fiction in the past tense. You're going to be relating a story that started some time ago—minutes, or millennia, it doesn't matter—and that moves, through an escalating sequence of events, toward some conclusion. That's why "Once upon a time" has been around so long—it sets us up nicely for a straightforward, linear narrative, at the same time that it promises us a surprising journey.

But lately it's become fashionable to tell some stories in the present tense. "Jack goes to the counter and orders a baloney sandwich. He eats it outside. He wonders where baloney comes from." Frankly, I find most such present-tense stories to be about that gripping. The idea, of course, is that the story will have a "You are there!" quality, a spontaneous, realistic, unfolding-before-your-very-eyes feel. Ann Beattie says, "Present tense gives the illusion of being hands-off; just tracking, like a camera." But of course it's *not* hands-off any more than any other tense, it's not unfolding right then and there—at least no more than any other story labored over and sent to a publisher. So, most of the time, and with wonderful exceptions such as James Salter's *A Sport and a Pastime*, and John Updike's *Rabbit, Run*, I personally find the pre-tense precious and vaguely annoying.

Where this present-tense approach does work, however, is in first-person stream of consciousness, pioneered by writers such as James Joyce. I defy anyone to read the interior monologue at the end of the short story "The Dead," included in the book *Dubliners*, and not be moved by its music and the imagery of snow falling, faintly falling, all over Ireland that night. Katherine Anne Porter does a bang-up job with it, too, in her short story, "Flowering Judas," told from the point of view of an adventurous young American woman getting mixed up with revolutionaries in Mexico City.

When it comes to screenplays, they are written in the present tense, always, but that's because we're not really meant to read them; they're a series of images and scenes and lines of dialogue designed for translation to the screen. Although some are indeed well-written, they're not meant to be literature; they're meant to be blueprints for the finished product, a movie that we will watch while munching our overpriced popcorn. (And why is it that even the best popcorn you make at home just doesn't taste as good? It's like the hot dogs you get at the baseball stadium. But I digress ...)

Present tense also comes in handy when it comes to technical or science writing. You don't want to know where the screw *went*; you want to know where it *goes*. And when you're writing, say, about the behavior of subatomic particles, you're writing under the assumption that the little buggers are acting the same way, right now, as they always have (not that we're ever quite sure) and that they'll go on doing it forever. The electron didn't *spin* around the nucleus; it *spins* around it.

Journalists employ it, too. If you're writing a profile, perhaps, of a breakout musical star, you might elect to use the present tense. You might want to say that she *strums* her zither with lacquered nails, not that she *strummed* it. It conveys the sense that the writer is right there, enchanted—as who would not be?—by the bewitching tones of the zither.

RULE 34.

PLANT NOW,
HARVEST LATER

Nobody likes a surprise. Not really. Once, someone threw a surprise party for me (a week *before* my birthday, so I didn't see it coming) and I've been in atrial fibrillation ever since.

And when you're writing fiction, or a screenplay, nobody likes it when the resolution to the story comes as a total surprise, either—when a character who has never been introduced suddenly appears out of nowhere to save the day, or when the climax is settled by some miraculous event like a heretofore unmentioned asteroid hitting the earth at precisely the right moment. It's a cheat, and your audience will take it that way. Aristotle identified this little trick, and it's generally called a deus ex machina, because, in Greek theater, gods could descend from Heaven to solve any intractable problem at the end of the play. The only hitch is, such unexpected and impossible-to-foresee interventions, if used in works done today, defy the internal logic of the story, and wreck the audience's willing suspension of disbelief.

Which isn't to say you can't ever use the occasional asteroid, or even a somewhat ancillary character, to give your story a shocking boost or twist at the end. But to play by the rules, you *must* have introduced, even in the most oblique way, that character earlier in the story; you *must* have suggested that such an element, whether it's an asteroid, or a dam that's about to burst, is lurking in the background somewhere, so that it doesn't come as a total shock when the ground shakes. This technique is generally referred to as "foreshadowing." Think of yourself as a farmer, sowing the seeds in the early parts of the story that will blossom or come to fruition much later on.

Sometimes, it's just a matter of suggesting something, almost in passing, that ultimately plays an important part in the story. I just watched a great old movie last night—*The Bridge on the River Kwai*—and in it, a young soldier, about to join a dangerous mission, is asked if, when it comes down to it, he thinks he could kill a man in cold blood, using a knife. He wavers, then says he thinks he can. Well, it turns out he can't, and that becomes a major plot point later in the film. It was not only an interesting note to give to the character, but the fact that it gravely affected the mission in the final reel makes it both satisfying and exciting. Trust me, audiences appreciate that kind of meticulous craftsmanship, even if most of them don't consciously recognize it. All they know is that the book or movie affected them, and that everything was neatly tied up in the end. It's other writers, however, who will definitely be more savvy—they'll see what you did, and salute you for it.

RULE 35.

SAY WHAT?

"What's wrong, Raoul?" she queried. "Don't you love me anymore?"

"I'm not sure," he opined.

"Is there," she speculated, "someone else?"

"It's not you, it's me," he expostulated. "And this terrible scene we're trapped in."

Can't say I blame him. But apart from the clichéd dialogue, what really makes the scene awful is all those ways the author (okay, that would be me) has found to avoid saying the word "said." And though I should no longer be surprised at this, I still come across writing manuals and instruction books, and even writing teachers, who encourage this kind of "creativity." One mail-away course, I kid you not, included this fine example of a way to avoid the dreaded "said": " 'I might jump,' he vacillated as he edged towards the cliff." And this was *recommended*!

In case no one has mentioned it before, I'm going to mention it now. The word "said" is an honorable one. It is, in every case, serviceable, and in almost every case, it is still the wisest choice for dialogue attribution. One of its greatest strengths is in its very ordinariness: no matter how many times you use it, it seldom, if ever, creates an annoying verbal echo in the reader's head. In fact, it hardly even makes a sound there. Readers don't hear it any more than they hear punctuation. It's just a silent signpost, making sure they're able to keep track of who's speaking to whom, so that they can attend to the more important things, like what your characters are actually saying to each other and what, below the surface, they might really mean. And that, of course, is where you want their attention, anyway.

Every time you search for a more interesting word than "said," and there are plenty of them out there, you run the risk of diverting the reader's attention, even momentarily, and of diminishing the efficacy and speed of the dialogue exchange. Sure, you can say, "he pleaded," "she demanded," and both of those verbs might add to the power of the scene—but they also might not. In almost every instance, "said" would have served, and if the scene is built well, so that we know who the characters are and what the discussion is about, we'll be able to gather the tone of voice just from the context.

Try this. The next time you're telling a story to a friend about what happened to you at work, or in class today, listen to hear how many times you say that someone declared, declaimed, admitted, confessed, announced, asserted, stated, or exclaimed, as opposed to the number of times you simply say "he said," or "she said." If it's good enough when you're simply telling a story, it should also be good enough when you're writing one.

RULE 36.

SHOW WHAT YOU KNOW.

No matter how mundane you think your job is, to someone else it's interesting.

No matter where you grew up, even the most undistinguished of middle-American suburbs, to someone else it's unusual.

No matter how ordinary you think your family is, trust me on this one—to other people, it's bizarre.

It is all, as they say, in the telling.

The things you take for granted, the local landscape, the climate, the way that people talk, the way they live their lives, is—or at least it can be—downright intriguing to people who lead their lives elsewhere, in other fashions. Did you grow up on the Great Plains, in a town with two silos, a feed store, and a single diner? It might have been boring as bricks to the teenage you, but to someone who grew up on Park Avenue in New York it might as well be Timbuktu. Do you now work as a mid-level functionary in the municipal housing office? To you, it might seem the most colorless of occupations; to others, it might provide an interesting glimpse into the workings of City Hall (*and* explain why their property taxes are as high as they are). Were you raised in a single-parent home, by your father, a fireman who moonlighted as an exotic dancer for bachelorette parties? (Wait—that one sounds like a Netflix series in the making.) Any or all of these things—the substance of your life, the stuff you know in your very bones and fiber, the things you accept as so normal they are beneath real notice—all of those things are offbeat and weird to others, and, if written about with unruffled fidelity, they can make for a fascinating tale.

For Jane Austen, who led what many of us would think of as a circumscribed life, the slice of English society that she did observe and explore, with such insight and acuity that her books have endured to this day, was all that she needed; she called it "polishing her little two-inches of ivory." Barbara Pym, another of my favorite English authors, wrote about jumble sales at the vicarage, and lonely spinsters in country towns, but again, she did it with such intelligence and sensitivity that her books can enthrall a guy like me, whose own life could not have been further removed from that milieu. We read those books for their truthful accounts of other worlds and eras, while we recognize in their stories, and their characters, the same emotions and human interplay we see in our own lives and relationships.

People read for two reasons: One, to go places they've never been before—Shangri-La or Paris in the spring, ancient Egypt or a Persian palace. And two, to go places they've already been a million times but have never seen rendered into art, places they have never had revealed to them as acutely as you, the writer, have been able to do. Your imagination can take your audience anywhere you feel like taking them—Applebee's or the Antarctic. Sometimes they'll be up for a rollicking ride to the other side of the globe, and sometimes they'll be perfectly happy to just hang around the house with you.

RULE 37.

MAKE 'EM CARE.

But may I return, for one moment, to Barbara Pym, whom I just mentioned, the late author of a dozen or so slim little novels set in mid-twentieth century Britain?

Nobody in these books is a dashing English lord with a dark secret. None is a ravishing beauty, with an insatiable lust for money and fame. There are no brutal murders, no ticking bombs, no high political skull-duggery or perilous adventure. And yet, these books can be as gripping as any page-turner churned out by John Grisham or Gillian Flynn.

What's her secret?

In a word, it's her characters. And in another word, it's the empathy she generates in us for them.

Pym so expertly takes us into the lives of her heroines, into their private desires and longings, their hopes and their fears, that we begin to feel those dreams and defeats, those hesitations and reservations, ourselves. We begin to root, ardently, for these humble characters to get what they want, even if what they want is for the vicar to accept their invitation to tea, or for their contribution to the bake sale to be singled out for a prize. The stakes are, by the standards of commercial fiction, never all that important—the fate of nations never hangs in the balance, the presidency is never threatened, the serial killer is not going to strike again—but the excitement runs high, nonetheless. It runs high because we have become invested in the people she has invented, and we want to see their modest hopes achieved, their unspoken longings addressed.

That, he said as if it were easy, is all you have to do. Create characters that your readers care so deeply about that anything that happens to them *matters*. To do that, however, you have to write about them honestly, clearly, and with a kind of compassion (even for the less-sympathetic ones). If *you* feel for them, there's a very good chance your readers will, too. And once that's done, the rest falls into place—we *care* whether or not they make the cheerleading squad, we *care* that they find their lost dog, we *care* about what's going to happen if they don't come up with the rent money.

The stuff of drama doesn't necessarily reside in White House intrigue, or Beverly Hills luxe. Guns don't have to go off, bodies don't have to drop, the sex doesn't have to be hot and kinky (not that there's anything wrong with that); drama is generated when those characters we care about must struggle to get what they want. The more we empathize and identify with them, the more they live and breathe in our imaginations, then the more we'll worry about them and turn the pages to find out what happens next. In the right hands, the saga of one young woman trying to find a place for herself in an indifferent city (see *Sister Carrie* by Theodore Dreiser) can be more enthralling than any wild and woolly international caper.

RULE 38.

FLAW YOUR HERO.

Heroes, by the way, don't have to be heroic.

In fact, the best protagonists, the ones that make a lasting impression, are decidedly not.

If you're writing about a central character who's virtuous, kind, strong, brave, handsome, well-mannered, with a sterling credit rating and a healthy respect for women, animals, trees, and cultural diversity, you are writing about a stiff, a guy too good to be true. And if he ain't true, he ain't believable, and if he ain't believable, why should we care what happens to him? *Nothing* can happen to him—he's a cartoon, and we all know that in cartoons, the characters can hold exploding bombs in their hands and emerge with nothing but smudged faces and spiky hair. They're indestructible, hence uninteresting.

A good hero or heroine is flawed. He has some failings, some things in his nature that aren't so admirable or likable; maybe your character, though essentially good-hearted, was brought up in an impoverished home, and as a result, is a bit of a skinflint. Maybe your heroine, though courageous and resourceful, is also willful and irresponsible, and her behavior winds up putting herself, and others, into some dangerous spots.

Maybe your protagonist has even got some nasty habits. John Self, the hero of Martin Amis's *Money*, is a drunk, a liar, a chain-smoker, a philanderer, a slob, a spendthrift. But because he is drawn with such humor and affection by the author, we end up laughing with him, and even hoping he will get out of the many scrapes that his bad habits get him into.

Mario Puzo's eponymous godfather, Don Corleone, is not a good man, either. He's a gangster, making his money off gambling, prostitution, extortion, etc. But tell me you don't root for him? Tell me you don't want things to go his way? One useful trick that Puzo employed, by the way, is worth mentioning. While he admittedly made his hero—first the Don, then Michael his son—bad guys, he made the other guys somehow worse. The kinky Senator, the Sicilian drug dealer, the sadistic police captain, the pedophile producer. Most of the time, Puzo keeps your allegiances firmly on the wrong side of the law, but because of the expert way in which he has created his characters and manipulated the drama, you don't feel violated or betrayed.

Because your reader must see antiheroes, like these, completely in the round, in all their human frailty, they are the hardest to create and render sympathetic. We have to feel we really know them, before we can move past their evil deeds, bad attitudes, and reprehensible conduct and, ultimately, forgive, and even embrace, them.

When creating your own hero, it's not a bad idea to keep the hero sandwich in mind—in other words, put in a lot of the expected things, and then add a few surprises. Sure, you can toss in the salami and provolone, but don't neglect the olives and red peppers and special condiments. Your hero has to be someone so winning as to hold our allegiance, but spicy enough to hold our interest, too.

RULE 39.

PERFECT YOUR VILLAIN.

By the same token, your bad guys can't be all bad, either. If they are, then they, too, become cartoons, malevolent machines whose actions and desires become predictable, linear, and, as a consequence, boring.

The monster in Mary Shelley's *Frankenstein* is a lumbering, lethal beast, but if that were all he was, the name of that book wouldn't even ring a bell today. Instead, Shelley created a character more sinned against than sinning, a creature that we, as readers, know has no viable place on this earth, built as he is from the body parts of the dead. But we are made to feel sympathy and even sorrow for him. (And by the way, if you are relying on the old Boris Karloff movies for your impression of the monster, then you are doing yourself a grave disservice: The book is still wonderfully readable, and the creature is far more complex, and even eloquent, than any movie version has given him credit for.)

If your antagonist is simplistic, monomaniacal and flat, then you're not giving your protagonist much to do, either. For your hero, it's the difference between playing tennis against a backboard—boring—and against a living, breathing opponent, someone capable of hitting the surprising drop shot or overhead lob back at him. A good villain brings out the best in your hero, forcing him to use all of his own wiles and courage in order to gain the victory.

If you understand your antagonist, and you give him something more in the way of personality than a single broad streak of menace, then one problem you won't have is in letting him come to life and speak his mind. For centuries, readers and critics alike have noted that the best lines in Milton's *Paradise Lost* go to Satan. The great villains—Simon Legree in *Uncle Tom's Cabin*, Inspector Javert in *Les Misérables*, Bill Sykes in *Oliver Twist*, Iago in *Othello*, Hannibal Lecter in *The Silence of the Lambs*—lend weight and power and meaning to the story; without them in fact, there would be no story.

In fact, some of the top-notch villains are those who absolutely believe in their own rectitude; *they* don't think they're *bad*. They think they're *good*. And in response to such characters, the reader gets to experience all the emotions of anger, indignation, revulsion, and dread that are no fun in real life, but a blast when they're inspired by a book or movie. He also gets to experience all the relief, even joy, that comes at the end of the story when the forces of evil are defeated and the world is put right again. (Assuming, of course, that it is. You're under no such obligation.)

As the writer, you get an added benefit when it comes to villains: They're so much fun to write. There it is, I've said it. Milton knew it, Shakespeare knew it, Emily Brontë knew it. (If her Heathcliff isn't the epitome of the dark and dangerous romantic hero, then I don't know who is.) With the hero, even a suitably flawed one, you still have to keep an eye on his likeability, his values, and, especially these days, his political correctness. (Just lighting a cigarette can make him a shady character in some readers' eyes.) But with the antagonists, you have none of those worries—villains can smoke, drink, lie, carouse, not to mention steal, pillage, swindle, commit murder. Not only that, they're *encouraged* to be bad. A villain whose worst crime is stealing hubcaps is not going to work up much emotion in your readers—or, for that matter, in you. If your characters—good or bad—don't inspire strong feelings, one way or the other, in you, their creator, then there's not much chance they'll do it in folks who just stumble across them in the pages of your book, or up there on a movie screen.

To write these bad guys, you are going to have to get in touch with your dark side—which, for many writers, isn't easy. We write to enlighten, to amuse, to entertain our audience, and the very notion of creating evil—even in imaginary form—can seem foreign or wrong. As a result, the antagonists can wind up as pushovers or cardboard cutouts. That's why it's especially important, when developing them, that you put in the same amount of effort and thought that you did in creating their virtuous counterparts. Give your villains a background, a backstory, and all the humanizing traits you can stand. We'll hate them all the more for it.

RULE 40.

SKIP THE TRUTH.

The truth, you've undoubtedly heard, can set you free.

Well, it can also tie you into knots.

If you're writing a biography, a serious scientific paper, a company report, then by all means let the truth be your guide. (Or try to.)

But if you're writing an imaginative work—a novel, a story, a screenplay, even a memoir—the most dangerous thing you can do is worry too much about a silly old thing like the truth.

When I've been teaching writing courses, many's the time I've been presented with a work in which something highly improbable or unconvincing appeared, and when I brought it to the writer's attention, he or she shot back, "But that's what really happened!" It's said in all earnestness, as if the truth were the best defense, and as if, just because the incident actually occurred, it had to be rendered exactly as it went down—no matter how undramatic, unlikely, or fundamentally irrelevant that was. If something truly that strange occurred, then it's your job, if you include it, to address the improbability factor head-on and persuade us of its authenticity. And even then, only if it's that significant. Whether you're writing a work of fiction, or a nonfiction account of, say, a nightmarish family car trip, your first allegiance is not to the truth, but to your audience. Make us *believe*.

And edit. If all we wanted to read was a blow-by-blow account of that dreadful car trip, we'd ask for a complete transcript and a copy of the itinerary. But that's not what we want.

Writing is an act of distillation, of separating the wheat from the chaff, and, most important of all, giving shape to the shapeless. In life, one thing follows another, seldom with any apparent logic, and sometimes without any clear causation. In art, we have to impose that logic, we have to give the audience a sense that things happen for a reason, and that they happen *in a certain order* for a reason. Is this lying? Sure—all art is a lie. But it's a lie told in the service of a greater truth. Even a photograph doesn't capture the truth—it captures what one photographer, with one camera in her hands, perceived and recorded in one split second. What did she get in the frame? How did she compose it? What did she leave out (that you'll never know or see)?

In the same way, every time you choose one word over another, you've subtly altered the truth and how your readers will understand it. Every time you rearrange the words you're using to describe an incident, you're changing the incident; you've messed with reality, with "what really happened." But far from feeling bad about it—or, even worse, beholden to the historical record—you should go right ahead and do it again. As an artist, *that's your job*—to take the raw material and sculpt it into something powerful and whole. Maybe something hard to believe really *did* happen—but that's no reason we should have to believe, or accept, it as is. Mold it for us into a plausible narrative event, and maybe then we'll go along for the ride. Maybe then we'll be able to get past the mere facts and see the truth.

RULE 41.

STRIP DOWN TO
YOUR BRIEFS.

If you've already heard this anecdote, forgive me.

But the eminent French philosopher Pascal once wrote a long letter to a friend, apologizing at the end for its length. He didn't have time, he explained, to make it shorter.

Ring any bells? There isn't a writer on the planet who hasn't written a few extra words now and then, who doesn't need to read over his or her work and do some judicious pruning. And when it comes to the heartfelt stuff, like letters and memoirs, the problem is only exacerbated. Who wants to stop midstream to start clearing up the clutter and editing the revelations pouring forth like water from a secret spring? Better to let it flow—we all know how hard it is to come upon a gusher—and worry about the cleanup later.

But worry about the cleanup, we must. When you write something needlessly wordy and convoluted, there's a reason for it—and that reason is usually a lack of clarity and purpose going in. Something in you—an impulse to get some thoughts down on paper, an urge to vent or passionately communicate your feelings about something—took hold, and so you started writing. So far, so good. There's gold in that rushing stream, but to find it you'll have to do some careful panning.

Only after you run out of breath and read over everything you've written will you really be able to see, and extract, the point and the pith of what you were saying. Writing long is easy, because you're not really doing one of the hardest things about writing—which is editing—as you go. Writing long is a way of searching for the truth, or the argument, as you go along, and asking the reader to accompany you on the ride. You may be able to make the trip so diverting she doesn't mind. Or—and this is, sadly, more likely—you may leave her stranded by the side of the road, halfway to the intended destination, wondering what that was all about and where, if anywhere, she was supposed to be going. Writing long is a perfectly good way to explore every avenue of thought, every possible turn in the road, every available sight along the way. There's a lot to be said for letting your typing fingers or scribbling pen outpace your conscious intellect, your inner censors, and even your more considered judgment. But once that's been done, it's wise to retrace your journey, Google Maps in hand, and figure out what, after all, would have been the most direct route.

RULE 42.

GO SUBLIMINAL.

Of the many reasons to write, one of the strongest is the urge to send a message, to communicate some strongly held view you have and, by so doing, open the eyes of the world to a great injustice. (And maybe, just maybe, doing something to correct it.) Harriet Beecher Stowe did it when she wrote *Uncle Tom's Cabin*. Upton Sinclair did it when he wrote *The Jungle*. John Steinbeck did it when he wrote *The Grapes of Wrath*. Rachel Carson did it when she wrote *The Silent Spring*. Betty Friedan did it when she wrote *The Feminine Mystique*.

You might be the next.

But when you're writing with a message in mind, you have to be careful. It's one thing if it's nonfiction—there you're entitled to write a polemic, full of sound and fury, statistics, examples, and complex arguments on behalf of your cause. The same for editorials, or their junior cousins, the ubiquitous letter to the editor. Make your case as boldly and convincingly as you can, using all your powers of persuasion and every trick you can pull out of your bottomless writing bag.

But if you're planning to convey your message in some other way—through, for instance, fiction—then you have to tread very carefully. People who read an editorial are expecting one thing; people who pick up a novel are expecting quite another. People who read an editorial are expecting to be informed, confronted, even hectored; people who read fiction are expecting, no matter how serious the subject matter, on some level to be entertained, or transported. They're not planning to attend a debate; they're planning to enter another world, an imaginary world, created and populated by you, the author, and in which they hope to lose themselves for a few hours, even a few days. If they wanted to pick a fight, they'd go to the local bar; if they wanted to educate themselves about the inequities of global food distribution, they'd log on to the appropriate website or go to an open lecture at a nearby university.

The pact you make, when you ask a reader to pick up your work of fiction is to deliver a *story*, an imaginative, cohesive (which doesn't mean it always has to be immediately coherent) tale. If there's an underlying message—that we don't do enough for the homeless, that the war on drugs does more damage than the drugs do, that racism is as endemic as ever—that's fine, but the message shouldn't be baldly stated. The reader shouldn't feel like he's been bludgeoned over the head, or even panhandled on the street. He should simply leave the world of your fiction with a greater insight into the subject you were writing about, and perhaps a greater fellow feeling for the people buffeted by the adverse forces you've described. Your readers should be first-class passengers on the plane of your narrative, traveling unaware of the heavy cargo that's being transported all the while, unseen, in the hold.

COOK UP A STORY.

Not long ago I went to a public event sponsored by a local community college, where unpublished writers could read aloud from their works in progress. And while I did not expect to be bowled over by the offerings, I did come away shocked—shocked by how uniformly *good* the selections were. The prose I heard that night was carefully wrought and often beautifully expressive, and though I had planned to stay only half an hour or so, I wound up sitting there, on that hard folding chair, for the full evening.

But I did start to miss one thing. In all these skillfully rendered selections, there was little, if any, sense of movement, of change. Everything was extraordinarily well observed and described, but that alone seemed to be the point of the writing—to capture a scene, a moment, a fleeting mood. The pieces I heard that night seemed, by and large, to be in stasis, or something darn close to it. If there was any conflict, it was in a distinctly lower key; if there was any change in a character's situation, it was so modest as to be almost imperceptible. If anything actually happened, it was off-screen, downplayed, or barely acknowledged.

Now, not everything we read needs to be plot-driven; not everything needs to be Daniel Silva or Tana French. But I must admit that when I hear the work of hugely popular authors like these disparaged or diminished, I want to spring, quite unnecessarily, to their defense. Building a story that keeps readers turning the pages, creating a narrative structure with a sense of momentum, where one event leads to another, and the final outcome remains in doubt, is a remarkable feat—and the reason that these writers get paid such princely sums to keep doing it.

With all the attention to fine writing these days, and the myriad creative writing programs in high school, college, and beyond, it's easy to focus on the art of writing, on nuances of language and the graceful evocation of mood. But at the same time it's critical that you keep that sturdy old workhorse called *Story* firmly in your sights. If your story

doesn't *have* much of a story, it's likely to remain inert. All those characters you've so lovingly created have nothing to do. All your clever
dialogue in the end has little to convey. All your well-crafted scenes
don't accrete or lead on to one another—they simply exist like spar-
kling gemstones that remain unstrung, never having found a common
thread. But find a solid story and you will bring them all together into
one truly fabulous piece of jewelry.

RULE 44.

LET THEM LEAD THE WAY.

Rumor has it that a writer died and left instructions that his tombstone should be inscribed with the words, "At last, a plot!"

Which just goes to show you how tough it is to come up with one.

Lord knows I've beaten my own head against the wall for countless hours in search of good, fresh, ingenious plots. And I've been told, as no doubt have you, that there are no completely original ones left. There are, according to whichever authority you listen to, three main plots, or six, or a dozen, and everything else is just a minor variation on one of them. And maybe it's true. What I do know is that every plot you come up with will, at some point, start to remind you of some other plot in a book you've read or a movie you've seen. Read enough, see enough flicks, and before long you'll have such a wide frame of reference that virtually everything you think of will bounce off, or call to mind, some story you're already familiar with. Eventually, you may despair of ever finding anything new.

But maybe that's because you're overheating your dynamos. Instead of trying to come up with some big idea—a ticking bomb on the president's plane, a deadly plague, a cop who can tap into the mind of serial killers—try thinking small. Try thinking, specifically, of your characters, not your plot. If you're not sure what the action of your story should be, forget about it for a while, and focus instead on the people involved. No matter how strong a plot is, or how "high-concept" it is in the Hollywood parlance, it won't amount to much, anyway, if the characters aren't engaging or memorable.

So, sit back and relax. Visualize your characters. Who are they? What do they look like? What are their hopes, their fears, their desires? And how will getting what they want somehow put them into conflict with others? I've seen it recommended that you create a whole backstory and bio for all your characters—where they went to school, how many siblings they had, what their favorite pet was, etc. If it works for you, go for it. Personally, I've always been too lazy (and, frankly, there are days when I can barely remember how many siblings *I* have or where *I* went to school.) But I do try to figure out what will set my characters into motion, how they will wind up colliding, and what will happen as a result of that collision.

If even that doesn't work, then I take a different tack. I think about introducing a new or different character; sometimes it just takes adding something to the mix—a nasty boss, or a flirtatious neighbor, an overbearing mother or a long-lost sister—to kick the story into gear. And because the action evolves from the peculiar interactions of characters that only you could have brought to life and to the page, and not from some mechanical and superimposed plot, it'll all sound and feel original. Daunting though it may be, plot is really nothing more than credible characters bumping up against each other and, ideally, leaving some kisses and some complaints, some bruises and some blessings.

RULE 45.

MAKE AN ENTRANCE.

Short of poetry, screenwriting is probably the most economical form of writing. Every word counts because there aren't supposed to be any superfluous words at all—the script is supposed to be as lean and clean as a blueprint.

And it was from a veteran screenwriter that I learned one of the paramount rules of his trade, when I was on staff at a TV show and writing my first episode. "Always arrive late, and leave early," he said, and though at first I rejoiced, thinking he was talking about the office hours, I soon learned that he was referring to the script I was working on.

It seemed, in retrospect, a good rule for pretty much any kind of writing.

Figure out what the action of the scene is going to be, or what its thrust is, and then backtrack just a smidgen, and start writing right there. In other words, if the scene takes place in a lecture hall, ask yourself if we really need to see the students filing in, the professor clearing his throat, the lecture being given, before we get to the crux of the matter—which is the argument that erupts between the professor and your protagonist, in which your protagonist is thrown out of school. If *that's* what the scene is about, if that's what moves the action of your story forward, then come in just before the argument flares up and out of control. And once the expulsion notice is given, end the scene—or "Cut!" as they say in the movie biz. Lingering in that lecture hall will only dilute the power of the confrontation.

Whatever you're writing, even if it's an article, an essay, a letter, there's an irresistible tendency to meander. And that's understandable in the first draft. But when you're doing the revision, look again at that prologue material and see how much of it you really need. Most of the time, you'll find that it's simply holding your reader at arm's length, and maybe, in the worst case, boring him to tears. It's like that guy at the bar, who takes so long to get to the point of his story that everyone's finished their drinks and emptied the peanut bowl and left by the time he does.

The same goes for knowing when to quit. When the action of the scene is completed, when the point has been made or the punch line delivered, do not hang around. Anything else you say at this point can only weaken what came before. Quickly look for the nearest exit, and go through it.

As I am doing now.

RULE 46.

DO DOUBLE DUTY.

And while we're borrowing from the screenwriter's bible, here's another little nugget that often serves well for other kinds of composition, too.

When you're writing a scene, look at the action. Look at what happens in the scene. Do a couple of your characters get in their car and drive across town to have dinner? Okay, fine, but now, ask yourself this: Is that *all* that happens in the scene? Do we manage to overhear the two discussing their respective days, or, better yet, bickering about where to eat? We're getting there. But look harder at the scene, and ask yourself again—is all we're seeing a drive, and a squabble?

If that's the case, then the scene is probably what we call, in the script business, shoe leather. That means it's a scene that accomplishes little more than, literally, getting some people from one place to another, or laboriously establishing some necessary plot point. To be blunt, if all that's happening in your scene is what's happening in your scene, then it probably isn't earning its keep. (I believe this rule, by the way, originated with the eminent screenwriter William Goldman—though it was first passed along to me by a producer I once worked for.) In other words, what you want to invest the scene with is some subtext, an emotional or thematic burden that gives the surface action some greater heft and purpose.

The surface action of the scene doesn't have to be anything special. In some ways, the more mundane it is, the better. Your characters can simply be playing cards (see the play *The Gin Game*), or motoring around town on errands (see *Driving Miss Daisy*), or discussing any ordinary, everyday matter at all (see almost anything written by Raymond Carver, Frederick Barthelme, Ann Beattie or Richard Russo). It's while they're going about these routine things that they are simultaneously revealing important things about themselves, about each other, and about the way in which they view the world. It's not in the overt actions of the scene, or even in the dialogue per se—it's in the things that are left undone, the words left unsaid, the evasions and elisions, the hesitations and prevarications and unexpected gestures. In Paddy Chayefsky's brilliant screenplay for *Marty*, Marty and his pals regularly ask each other, "What do you want to do?" It's the flattest, most desultory conversation imaginable, and yet the repeated plaint comes to painfully suggest the depths of the loneliness and aimlessness of the guys' lives. It's a poignant cri de coeur disguised as an offhand remark, and it's writing at its simplest and at its most sublime.

RULE 47.

BE A TEASE.

In all writing, as in love, it pays to be a coquette.

Whatever your message is, whatever you set out to convey to your reader, it's never a good idea to deliver too much, too soon. Your reader is not only unprepared, but he or she can be, quite frankly, disappointed.

If someone's reading your editorial, she wants to be persuaded. She wants to see your argument unfold, and your conclusion reached, as if inexorably, by the irrefutable train of logic you have presented. Even if ultimately she chooses to disagree, she wants to understand where you started and how you got there—if only to write her own scathing rebuttal the next day.

If it's fiction, then your reader needs time, and pages, to acclimate himself to your world and get his bearings. Throw too much at him too quickly—an exotic locale, a wide cast of characters, an abundance of action—and he may feel overwhelmed and unable to catch up. If this sensation lasts too long, he'll find some easier way to occupy those precious leisure hours. (If there's one thing that causes me to put down a novel after just five or ten pages, it's when I get that feeling I've stumbled into a huge family gathering, where everyone else is right at home, catching up and swapping stories, and I know no one in sight. I grab one last cheese puff and head for the door.)

Suspense is a necessary component of any writing; without it, we'd never go from one sentence to the next. Even in a letter to a friend, you are creating some kind of narrative, a concatenation of events (I love that word, "concatenation"—just say it out loud and catch the rhythm) that will carry your friend along. You're building a story, or an anecdote, or a scene from your recent vacation, bit by bit, and as you add each detail, the picture becomes more complete. But the art of that is as much in the withholding, as it is in the divulging.

Every time you choose what to write next, you are holding back something else; you are essentially putting things in order—first in your head, and then on the page. Whenever you hit a snag in your work—especially while writing nonfiction or journalism—you can often trace it back to something you said too soon, without having set it up properly or having put it in the proper context. As a result, other things have begun to pile up in an unseemly pile, and you soon find yourself trying, with increasing desperation, to straighten it all out. Unfortunately, the more you flail around, the worse things usually get. It's far better, in general, to go back and pinpoint where you jumped the gun. Then, after you've taken a long and calming breath, you can crouch down in the starting blocks again, and prepare to run that leg of the race all over.

RULE 48.

KEEP THE FAITH.

In some ways, this—keeping the faith—is the hardest of all the problems any long-form writer faces.

If all you're writing is an editorial, a short essay, even a brief article, you can do it in one or two sittings. In fact, the best think pieces, to my mind, are the ones that do spring from one session, as if exhaled in one breath. They usually have a clarity and a consistency of tone, a wholeness, that long-aborning pieces often lose.

But a book or a screenplay requires a sustained effort, over months, even years, and, consequently, a delay in the ultimate gratification—of publication, or production. Your editorial may appear in the paper the next day, and your friends may text you dozens of nice comments. But your book may take years to appear on a shelf; your screenplay may take years to get produced and shown in theaters or streamed on the latest trendy site. And during all the time that you're working, all those same friends will drive you mad with well-meaning questions like, "So how's the book coming? When can I buy a copy?" and "Who's going to be starring in the movie? Will it be out in time for Christmas?" (Truth be told, I don't think all those queries are so innocent; some, I suspect, are meant to be pointed as needles, deftly inserted to give you a twinge.)

But such questions will have their effect, and chiefly because they echo the same questions ringing in your own head. When *will* this thing ever be done? *Have* I been wasting my time? Is it worth all this trouble and energy? What, exactly, was it supposed to be about? (And why doesn't it seem to be about that anymore?)

You have come, with apologies to Dante, to that "dark wood where the straight way is lost." You have lost your faith along with your bearings. And you wonder if you will ever get either one of them back again.

You will.

Your bearings will come back more quickly. Merely taking that break, recommended earlier, will probably open your eyes to the technical problems, and to their solution.

Your faith, well, that's trickier, isn't it? It's a real conundrum. To get it back, you just have to believe—in yourself, your work, your mission. One thing that might help is knowing that virtually every other writer writing has encountered these same problems, has entertained these same doubts, has dropped his or her head onto the desk and wondered why it wouldn't be a better idea, after all, to take up scrapbooking or bird-spotting. (Could it be that all those avid scrapbookers and amateur ornithologists are, in fact, blocked writers?) And some writers, it's true, have given up. I cannot tell a lie.

But most of them—like you, my hearty—eventually remembered what drove them to do this in the first place, the impetus that set them on their way. The spark that started the fire is still glowing, and all it takes to bring it again into flame is a breath or two of air. And wouldn't it be a shame to let it die down now, what with all those pages already done, all those pages that your friends secretly believe you never wrote, sitting in the cardboard box under the desk? (I know, you can simply save things to the Cloud and all that, but I still believe that at any moment, civilization will collapse, and with it the internet and every other technological development, and we will be back to using parchment and quills—and I'm okay with that. So, save a hard copy somewhere.)

But if nothing else, don't you want to be able to wave a published book under the noses of those doubting Thomases one day? Wouldn't that be sweet? Can't you just taste it? Nobility is fine, but the baser instincts should never be underestimated as a spur to higher purpose.

RULE 49.

FLY SOLO.

After many years of writing all by myself (I was lucky if the even the dog wanted to join me), I was invited to join the staff of a TV show.

All of a sudden I was in a room with four or five other writers, whiteboards all around the walls covered with act breaks and script notes, and, most troubling of all, a bucket of M&M's and peanut butter cups, constantly replenished, in the center of the table. I gained six pounds in as many weeks.

What I also gained was an appreciation for other writers' ideas, points of view, and even their working methods. We would all pitch in on premises for the episodes, how the stories would affect our major characters, what the major turning points would be. And once a thorough outline was up on the boards, one of us would retire to a quiet office, and bang out a draft of the script. (One of many that would come thereafter, as I soon learned.)

While it was a relief to find myself making up stories with a lot of collaborators, there to bail me out whenever I hit a snag, I soon found the experience vaguely grating. I was used to having my own way—it's one reason writers become writers in the first place—and I chafed at having someone else overrule or rewrite me. Even if their ideas or changes were perfectly okay, I generally wanted to go with mine. In one memorable instance, a fellow writer kept sticking a gross joke into one of my scenes, and no matter how many times I removed it, he would find a way to sneak it back in on the next communal draft. It was ultimately cut, to the best of my recollection, but the experience was annoying.

So, as a writer you've got to ask yourself—are you a sole practitioner, or a team player? Personally, I discovered I'm a lone wolf. Sink or swim, I prefer to be my own captain and crew.

That said, there are some distinct advantages to collaborating, usually with one partner, when it comes to TV or film. That's where you see most of the collaborative temperaments and arrangements. Writing a comedy script, for instance, lends itself to a partnership. Did your joke make the other person laugh? Did your partner come up with something off-the-wall that knocked you out of your chair? Do you find that lines of dialogue fly back and forth between you like a badminton birdie? (I know one team who keeps a tape recorder running in their office at all times, just in case one of them says something great on the fly and the one at the keyboard can't keep up.)

Only once did I try collaborating, however reluctantly, on a novel. My friend and I had already written a screenplay that went nowhere, and then I said I'd take the plot and rewrite it as a novel. He insisted on sharing the labor, so we decided to each write a chapter and then swap them. In mine, I had written a sentence that read, in its entirety, "He stopped." My collaborator had neatly added, in the margin, "like a deer caught in the headlights." That's when I knew for certain that this collaboration was not going to work. As with every other aspect of writing, I prefer to pick out my own clichés.

RULE 50.

GO FOR BROKE.

As a national environmental policy, conservation is good.

It's even good as part of your daily life. Don't throw away items that still have utility.

But as a writing technique, it stinks.

I actually had a writing student who was full of colorful anecdotes and great story ideas in class, but whose written work never quite measured up. Sometimes that's just due to a lack of writing ability, but that wasn't the case here.

The stories she'd turned in were perfectly well written; they just weren't about very much, and they were nothing like the rich trove of material she'd share with me in office conferences, or even out loud in the classroom. When I finally asked her why she thought this was, she answered without a moment's pause, "Because I'm saving that stuff."

"Saving it? For what?"

"My novel."

I should have known.

Like many writers, she felt like she had to conserve her best material for that project that was always just around the bend. (She was already in her late twenties, so I don't think it would have been too hasty of her to spend a little of this precious literary capital.) The good stuff, to her way of thinking, was too good to waste on class assignments and schoolwork; it was destined for greater things, for the glittering showcase of a novel.

And while I'm all for writing novels, I am not for the pickling of literary material. For one thing, you may think you're saving it up for later use, but in fact you're letting it get stale, you're letting it lose some of its vitality. Material you think is unforgettable today you will have forgotten by this time next year.

Fortunately, by then you will have accumulated much more. Writers who fear using their best stuff are worried that there won't be any more where that came from. They're afraid that they're going to run out, when that, in fact, is the one thing you never have to worry about. As long as you're alive, you're accumulating new material all the time. Not to mention, perspective, insight, understanding. (You'll note that I don't say you *behave* any better; I do say that you might have a better notion of why you *mis*behave—and that at least is something.)

Conventional wisdom has it that we get more conservative as we get older, but I think the opposite is often true. (It certainly is in my case; although I was raised in a conventional Midwestern household, in another few years I'll be a raving, nudist, hippie throwback.) As we age, we learn to accept things that our parents may have taught us were unacceptable; we see things, even in our friends, that we may not condone, but that we learn to live with. We encounter adversity, in even the most otherwise blessed lives. We get a wider, more experienced, all-encompassing view of life, and that view informs everything we write, adding scope and depth and empathy—empathy most of all—to the work. Our best material gets even better, and the more we use of it, the more of it we miraculously seem to have.

RULE 51.

LAY DOWN THE LAW.

Nobody likes a namby-pamby—and least of all in an author.

When you're writing, you're creating your own world on the page, and in that world you are God. So act it.

Readers don't need to agree with you, they don't even need to like you, but they do need to feel that you are in control of that world; they need to know that even if there isn't an actual wizard behind the curtain, there is an attentive author pulling all the levers and keeping things straight.

A few years back, there was a brief vogue in publishing circles for "make-your-own-adventure" books, books that contained alternate endings and left it up to the reader to choose among them. (I was even asked to write one of these.) Want a happy ending, where the lovers reunite? Choose Ending A. Want a more downbeat, perhaps realistic, conclusion? Choose Ending B, where they part at the train station, wiser but wearier.

These books failed, and for the very reason that I knew enough to turn down the one that was offered to me. Readers don't *want* to have to choose their own ending, any more than they want to have to choose their own beginning, or middle. If they could do all that, they'd write the books themselves, and they wouldn't need authors at all.

Writing is choosing—this word over that one, this twist instead of that turn. We read certain writers because we have come to trust and enjoy their choices—we know, when we read a tale by Dickens, that there's going to be a very large cast of characters, bafflingly intertwined, and that in the end everything will be sorted out for us. By the same token, when we read a lengthy article by one of our favorite journalists, we trust the writer to introduce us to her subject, guide us through the intricacies of her argument, and conclude in a memorable fashion. She's done it before—why not again?

Ambiguity is fine, in small doses. (Who among us was not assigned de Maupassant's "The Lady or the Tiger" in junior high?) But when we sit down to read a whole book, watch an entire movie, or plow through a substantial piece, we want to feel that the hand guiding us by the elbow is a firm one. Even the most open-minded, experimentally tolerant among us (and I'm not one) wants to know that somebody else has given this material a lot of thought, because if no one has, why should we spend our own time trying to unravel it?

Art can be as challenging as you want to make it—as challenging as you think your audience can stand. But remember that, ultimately, your readers are counting on you to lead them into the forest and then back out again, and the last thing they want to hear from you is, "Jeez, I don't know—where do *you* think we are?"

RULE 52.

KEEP YOUR PROMISES.

Your readers are counting on you for something else, too. They're counting on you to follow through on the promises you've made.

What promises? you may ask. *I barely know these people.*

Well, that doesn't matter. Any time you write something, and expect someone else to read it, you are making them a promise, of one kind or another.

If it's a travel article, you're promising to give them a thorough portrait of the place you're describing, and to leave them with sufficient information to decide whether or not they'd like to visit that place themselves one day.

If it's a think piece for the newspaper, you're promising to deliver a cogent argument, one that opens their mind to new possibilities.

If it's a movie script, you're promising to tell an involving story, one that has a beginning, a middle, and an end (preferably in that order), that ties up all the loose untidy plot strands and leaves your audience feeling satisfied.

Not to mention, the most fundamental promise of them all. Every time you start writing something, you are suggesting a deal: In return for the readers' time and attention, you are offering entertainment. It doesn't have to be crazy car chases or hot love scenes, but it does have to be interesting. It does have to take your readers somewhere they've never been, show them something they've never seen, teach them something they've never known. That's the implicit deal you've made, and your readers, even if it's never been spelled out, know it as well as you do.

When you finish a piece of work, and you've let it cool down, like a pie on the windowsill, read it over and look for all the issues you've brought up, the expectations you've raised, the plot points you've made. How well have you delivered on them all? In your editorial, did you play fair, and at least allude to the opposing point of view, before concluding your definitive argument? In your travel piece, did you remember to mention that this island paradise has a trifling problem with typhoid fever? In the screenplay, did you resolve all the major conflicts on which the story turned—or are moviegoers going to stop on the way back to their car, and say, "Well, wait a minute—did they get the diamonds or not?"

Don't break your promises. Keep them.

RULE 53.

SWEAT THE SMALL STUFF.

This may be painful, but I'd like to ask you to think back to your first, or simply most memorable, blind date. (Never had one? How'd you manage that?)

For the rest of us . . . remember what you noticed the moment you met the person and how instantaneously you formed your first impression? What was your date wearing? Tight designer jeans and a tube top? Or a neatly tailored, but severe business outfit? What was your date driving—a sleek silver Porsche, or a sensible, battleship-gray Honda Civic? Or maybe even a Harley with a flaming decal and those ridiculous raised handlebars?

Face it—you were making split-second judgments. You were categorizing that person based on simple signifiers like clothing and vehicles. And while you may have later learned that the Harley driver was actually a mild-mannered professor of literature, or the girl in the Peter Pan collar and conservative plaid skirt was a lingerie model, that first glimpse was telling.

That's why every detail, regardless of how small, matters when it come to creating a character. Whether you're making up a fictional human being for a story or a screenplay, or describing a real-live person that you have just interviewed for a personality profile, you have to choose, wisely but sparingly, the precise details that you include. Why? Because every reader of your book, or viewer of your movie, is going to be doing just what you did on that first date—making assessments and jumping to conclusions about these people based on the clues you've provided. If your character shows up in a Rolls-Royce, we'll assume she's rich, unless you tell us otherwise. If your character shows up wearing a goatee and paint-spattered coveralls and a loose bandanna, we'll assume he's an artist (or a bohemian housepainter). You never want to provide so many details that the picture gets confused; you want to provide just enough of the most salient ones to build up the picture of the person in your audience's mind.

One thing you don't want to do—and it is a pet peeve of mine—is give too many physical details about their face and even body. I had one friend—a successful paperback author—who introduced every character by height and weight. "Michael, standing six feet tall and weighing 184 pounds, greeted Angela, who was a foot shorter and weighed 123 pounds, at her door." I was forever trying to figure out if these people were meant to be in good shape or bad. Nor could I ever complete the mental portrait of those characters in Victorian-era novels whose faces were described as "a delicate oval, with a nose more aquiline than her ancestors, but nonetheless pointing upwards toward her eyes, which were an indeterminate shade of blue, though overshadowed by an unnecessarily protuberant brow and lashes of a length so great that they threatened to divert attention from her full, rose-red cheeks and closely situated conch-like ears." What the . . . ? In fiction, I think you should consider giving your characters a sketch rather than a full-scale oil portrait. Most readers will only remember a thing or two at most— that the guy has a gleaming bald head, or the woman has twelve piercings in her face—and then they'll fill in the rest for themselves. (That's why, when you see a movie of a book you've read, the characters never look anything like how you pictured them.)

Finally, never cheat by having a character look in the mirror in order to shoehorn in a physical description—"He studied his face in the shaving mirror, noting his firm jaw and thrice-broken nose"—or by comparing them to movie stars. That same friend who described everybody by height and weight also liked to do that—"She was the spitting image of Jennifer Garner, but from her days on the show *Alias*, when she stood roughly 5-foot-seven and tipped the scales at a scanty 119 pounds." Forget the celebrities—and the scales.

RULE 54.

HIT YOUR MARKS.

The worst editors I know are the ones who assign you a piece, and then, when you ask them how long they want the piece to be, say, "Oh, let's just see what it comes in at."

Mostly, this happens at magazines and newspapers, but it can be a problem with whatever you're working on. Why?

Because length matters. (No jokes, please.)

The length of a manuscript, whether it's a magazine feature or a novel, determines a whole host of other practical and aesthetic decisions that you have to make along the way—and if, going in, you don't know what that length is supposed to be, you are laboring under a great handicap.

First and foremost, there is the question of pace. If you've been assigned, say, an article on how to buy a used car, you need to know how many words you're supposed to write because, without that number, you don't even know what kind of lede to write. If all you've got is 750 words, then you're going to start out with, and keep up, a very brisk pace—you're going to jump right into the piece, without preamble, and probably deliver your main points in a bullet style. But if, instead, you've got 2,500 words to squander, then you might decide to make your lede anecdotal—you might choose to introduce a lovely young couple, clutching their checkbook, timidly stepping onto the used car lot and hoping to emerge with the car they'd been dreaming of, and at a fair price. (Fat chance.)

Your style, throughout the piece, is going to differ, too, depending on the word count. Longer pieces allow, obviously, for a more effusive style (though they don't necessarily insist upon it). Shorter pieces require a quick, get-to-the-point approach. Again, it helps to know the score ahead of time.

Length also determines how and when, you deliver your important information. In the case of the used car article, for instance, you'll be wanting to touch on Bluetooth capabilities, rust-proofing, factory rebates, etc. And if you're writing short, all this stuff will be compacted and up front—bang, bang, bang, and you're out of there.

Writing long, these issues will be measured out, possibly in teaspoons. Every couple of hundred words, you should be taking on another major point or issue. And if you keep one eye on the finish line, you can always gauge the distance remaining, and either pick up, or slow down, your pace accordingly.

But what about when you're writing for yourself—"on spec," as they say? Isn't it a great comfort and relief not to have to worry about length, to just sit down and let 'er rip? Well, sure, and that is one of the beauties of writing without an assignment in hand, or an editor looking over your shoulder. The material dictates the length.

But in my experience, the material can also run amok. It can refuse all attempts to be reined in, governed, or even shaped. Without a clear idea of what you're writing—a slim memoir? a bulky family saga?—you don't know how to set your internal metronome. You don't know whether to set the pace at adagio or andante. Write a chapter, maybe two, and once you're satisfied with them, study their rhythm. That's the rhythm you probably want for the rest of the book, and it in turn will help you to define the length and the scope of the project. Just listen to the ticking.

RULE 55.

DON'T PUSH YOUR LUCK.

Okay, so you're having lunch with a friend, and complaining about your last boyfriend, when, of all people, who should come in and sit down at the very next table? The man himself—with a date.

"What a coincidence!" you might think (as you fumble for your steak knife.)

And, if you were to use this as a kick start for a story or a movie, it'd be perfectly okay. Coincidences do happen. That's why we have a word for them.

But they *don't* happen all that often. If they did, they wouldn't be coincidences anymore. They'd just be more of that random stuff that happens to us everyday.

When Ilsa walks into Rick's bar in *Casablanca*, that's a coincidence—such a whopper, in fact, that the script even acknowledges it by having Rick mutter, "Of all the gin joints in all the towns in all the world, she walks into mine." (In movie parlance, by the way, that's called "hanging a lantern" on it—openly admitting to something that might otherwise strain the credulity of the audience and distance them from the story. By pointing at it yourself, you've acknowledged the audience's question, shared it with them, and as a result, you can all put it behind you and move on from there.)

Audiences, and readers, will forgive you for using coincidence at the start of a story. It's sort of a given, a way that so many stories employ to set everything else into motion. If Ilsa hadn't walked into that bar, there'd *be* no *Casablanca*, and we would all have been the losers thereby. But, as the author, you have now spent your "coincidence capital." You've used your free pass, and another one is going to be awfully hard to come by.

If you really feel you have to—if your story provides you with no other way around it—and you just *have* to use another coincidence, then you should know that your audience is going to raise one very large and very skeptical eyebrow. They'll feel like you're cheating—and in a way you are.

With one small caveat. If your extra coincidence makes things *worse* for your hero—if the office worker playing hooky at the track bumps into his boss at the betting window, and then also collides with a gangster he owes money—it's more acceptable than if he bets on a winning horse and then meets the girl of his dreams. Don't ask me why, but misfortune feels more believable than good luck, and even carries a comic bite. Maybe it's just that people are more likely to believe that bad things can happen all the time, and maybe it's because the second bad coincidence has the salutary effect of making the story more difficult or dangerous for your hero. Who wants to read about happy breaks? Whatever the reason, keep your coincidences to a minimum—and, if you must use them, lean toward the unlucky ones. Everybody knows what those feel like.

RULE 56.

TAKE A WALK AROUND THE BLOCK.

What would a book for writers be without a chapter on those two most infamous words of all—writer's block? Heck, I don't even like to type those words. Not because I'm scared of them, but because I don't like to give them any greater credence than they already have.

Nonfiction writers, to begin with, seldom suffer from writer's block—for a fairly simple reason. If you're writing a biography, you can always move on to the next big chapter in your subject's life; if it's a book on military hardware, you can move from mortars to bazookas; if it's a monograph on Cézanne, you can address the next painting. The path ahead—or at least one *possible* path—is generally clear.

But if you're writing a work of imagination, you *can* get stuck. Suddenly, in the middle of a novel or screenplay, you can find yourself unsure of where to go next. Even if you've armed yourself with a fairly rigorous outline, it's easy to come up against a wall. And the more you try to press on through that wall, the more your head hurts, until you give up. In despair.

But take heart. Maybe the reason you're stuck is a *good* one. While it could just be low blood sugar, it could also be a signal of something more significant. If *you're* not sure what happens next, then maybe *your reader* isn't sure, either. And that might be a good thing. It might mean that your narrative is crying out for something big at this point, some unexpected development, some shift in tone or chronological jump. Your writer's block might not be a Stop sign—it might just be a Slow sign. It's telling you that more thought, rather than more typing, is required right now, that you've come to a kind of crossroads. Maybe something really exciting is about to happen, and it's simply going to take you some downtime to discover what that is.

But what if your block is so great that you can't even get started on *anything*? What if you approach your desk, kitchen table, or wherever you work, with the same joy you anticipate doing your taxes? That's a symptom of something deeper. While I'm not actually a psychiatrist (and am only playing one in this book), I think this kind of block often has a lot to do with issues of self-worth. Even if you can't hear the actual words, you're asking yourself, *Who am I to be writing this book? What do I have to say that hasn't been said? And who would ever publish something I've come up with?* You're leaping over everything else that has to come first—from sharpening your pencils to picking a name for your protagonist (much harder than you'd think)—and landing in a bramble-bush of doubts and fears and negativity. But none of these things is truly a "writer's block"—they're a "living and breathing block," and maybe that's worse, but doing your work, *any* work, is ultimately going to prove your salvation. Achievement is the one thing that trumps depression, every time.

Writers who are blocked aren't incapable of writing—they can still hold a pen in their hand, or sit at the keyboard. What they can't do is write as beautifully as they'd like, and that's what's stopping them. They put down three words, decide they're not Shakespeare, and tear them up. Do that enough times and you've got a very healthy block going. The celebrated critic Jacques Barzun once wrote, "Convince yourself that you are working in clay, not marble, on paper, not eternal bronze; let that first sentence be as stupid as it wishes." And the second and third ones, too. "No one," Barzun added, "will rush out and print it as it stands." If you can accept that fact—and many blocked writers can't—you'll stop trying to write for the ages, and you'll start working instead on the humble, and, yes, possibly disposable pages that most of us are fated to produce.

RULE 57.

LOSE YOUR FORM.

Most professional writers have a favorite form—short story, essay, play, novel—that they regularly employ to express themselves and their ideas. But every one of them moonlights now and then, and uses a different form when the occasion calls for it.

So why shouldn't you?

Ideas come in all shapes and sizes, and sometimes what's right for a magazine article is all wrong for a nonfiction book. What might work fine as a screenplay may not have the heft for a novel. What might make for a lovely essay may not be translatable into fiction. And if, while trying to write one of these things, you keep getting hopelessly stuck, it might be because you've simply chosen the wrong form. It's the old round peg in a square hole problem.

So what if, God forbid, your idea seems to want to become a play, and you've never written a play before? What if the short story threatens to swell into a novel? A lot of writers feel they either have to abandon the idea altogether, or, first, spend several years studying the demands and requirement of the foreign form, buy every relevant book on the market, take every pertinent course—maybe even enroll in a university program and get a degree in it! If you happen to know that you are immortal, go right ahead—you've got all the time in the world.

For the rest of us, however, it's not that easy. We hope to write, and even publish, our work in the span of a normal human lifetime. And we cannot become an expert in everything. Which is why it's important to remind ourselves that we already know a lot more than we think we do. For one thing, if your idea is begging to take shape as a play, then that may be because you've seen some plays (I bet you have!) and you can already imagine, albeit imprecisely, how this idea would work on the stage. By the same token, you've seen a lot of movies, which may be why your inner voice is insisting that something about this new idea of yours would lend itself neatly to the big screen.

Writers, to quote the eminent author and literary critic Cynthia Ozick, "[breathe] inside a blaze of words," and that's what makes them writers. Some of these words they have read in poems, some they have heard declaimed on Broadway, some have even been absorbed just from watching TV. (These days, with the plethora of great shows, that's more likely than ever before.) And whether the writers were aware of it or not, they were also imbibing the form that the words were embodied in. Drinking the wine, they could not fail to notice the bottle from which it was being poured. When a new form beckons to you, when you feel that tingle of excitement, mixed with trepidation, which comes from accepting a challenge, rise to it—don't run away. I'm not suggesting you fly blind, that you take *no* time to comprehend the strictures of the new form, but I am suggesting that a lifetime spent in that blaze of words has prepared you better than you know.

RULE 58.

SET AN ALARM CLOCK.

While you're at it, set two alarms.

One is to make sure that you get to your desk on time every day. Writing only gets harder the longer you stay away.

And set the other one ticking in your work. When you're constructing a plot, see if you can't install, somewhere deep in the heart of the machinery, a little ticking clock that's counting down, second by second, to a big showdown of some sort.

Screenwriters live and die by this rule—which is why you see so many stories where the cop has to find the killer before the next full moon, or the heroine has to convince her old boyfriend to break off his imminent wedding, or the scientists have to figure out how the planet Earth can avoid the asteroid due to collide with it in just thirty-six hours! But screenwriters are definitely onto something here. That ticking clock can add immeasurably to any imaginative work.

For one, it gives your story a thrust, a spine, a destination. You can always check your progress against the looming cataclysm or unavoidable event. Are your readers worrying about the big tennis tournament your heroine has absolutely got to win? The declaration of love she must make before it is too late? The deadly conspiracy she must uncover and foil before the world, as we know it, is lost?

Because if they're not, they should be.

And are you, the author, ratcheting up the action and the ante? Are you using that clock like a time bomb, ready to explode? Have you set in motion a sequence of events that inevitably, and with increasing tempo, will lead to a critical juncture, one where the central conflict of your story will be resolved, for better or for worse? Also called a climax, every good story should have one. And when you build that climax in, you have all the advantages conferred by advance planning— you can see it coming, you can plan everything else to contribute to it, and you can prep your audience so that they fully comprehend and appreciate the gravity of the event when you get them there. They'll know exactly how much is at stake—a lot!—and if you've done your job right, they'll be anxiously awaiting the outcome. They should be watching the action like the dropping of the ball in Times Square on New Year's Eve—riveted, shivering, and drunk with expectation.

for three months, passes the experience—I tell you, they finish only the rewarding all the public acclaim and adulation that is sure to come.

RULE 59.

FALL IN LOVE.

Before embarking on any substantial writing project, ask yourself this: Am I in love?

Because if you're not in love with your idea, you will have a very hard time seeing it through to completion.

If it's just some casual flirtation, you'll never be able to go the distance. You'll get tired, bored, restless. Something else will beckon to you, you'll chase after that instead, and the whole mad cycle will start all over again. Some projects may appeal to you because they are timely, or hot, or overtly commercial, and while there's nothing wrong with pursuing such stuff, it's never easy to maintain the necessary enthusiasm for them over the months, even years, that they can demand. Cheap thrills don't last.

Ah, but if it's true love, if the subject is one that truly speaks to your heart, then somehow you will find the will and the energy to see the project through to completion. If it's a story that you need to tell, then you'll find a way to tell it, no matter how many drafts you have to go through to get there. If it's a dream you want to share with the world, you'll find a way to make that happen.

And you will subscribe, as you must, to the theory of delayed gratification. Writing big things—like novels, biographies, screenplays—means working, sometimes for years, just to get the thing done. And then there's the wait to see the work go out into the world, as a book or a movie. Be forewarned, these are not quick-turnaround industries—movies take a long time to set up, shoot, and distribute; books take a long time to get sold, printed, and shipped. I recently learned, for instance, that my new, finished novel—all done and in need of no further editing, according to the publisher—will come out exactly thirteen months from now. Was I happy to hear it? No. But I've been around this track before, and I know that it's pointless to get agitated about it. The only thing to do is to start in on the next big project, to fall in love all over again, with something new, and let those thirteen months pass—as, experience tells me, they unfailingly do—before accepting all the public acclaim and adulation that is sure to come.

RULE 60.

GET REJECTED.

Into every writer's life, some rain must fall—though sometimes, be forewarned, it may feel more like a deluge.

You will send your work out—to agents, editors, publishers—and it will come back to you like a boomerang. Turned down, passed on, rejected.

It's a rite of passage, and the sooner you make your peace with it, the better off you'll be.

That's not saying you'll ever entirely get used to it. It's always a shock when somebody doesn't love your work. And it's easy to take it to heart—it feels like they're rejecting you, personally, and not the work. But they're not (unless, in fact, they *do* know you and for some reason you really *have* ticked them off). No, when your work is rejected, that's all that's happening here, and it could have been rejected for a whole host of reasons you will never even know about and that had nothing to do with the quality of the work itself. Your project might have conflicted with something else they already had in the pipeline, it might have been too long, or too short, for their needs, it might have simply struck the wrong tone for their market or audience. They might even be planning to go out of business in three months, though they haven't gone public with that information yet. (Happened to me once.)

So whatever kind of rejection slip you get, don't waste a lot of time trying to read anything into it. If it's a form rejection, it's a form rejection, and that's that. But even if it's personalized somehow, don't knock yourself out parsing every word and figuring out what the editor meant. Most of the time she didn't mean much; she was just trying to soften the blow.

But there's an old Jewish saying that's relevant here. "If one person says you look tired, don't worry about it. If two people say you look tired, lie down." The same goes for rejection letters. If one editor says your manuscript is wrong for some particular reason, that could just be her opinion. But if a second editor mentions the exact same thing, then lie down—and give the complaint some serious thought. I sent out a partial manuscript of a novel once, and when the first editor passed on it because it seemed somehow "comic-y" to her, I laughed it off. What did she know? But imagine my consternation when another editor, at a different house, also passed on it, saying it reminded her, uncomfortably, "of a comic book story." Now, unless these two had had lunch and discussed it, which seemed extremely unlikely, I had to concede that there just might be something vaguely comic bookish about it, after all. (Truth be told, I'd seen it in my mind's eye as a cheesy movie in the vein of *Catwoman*, and I guess they'd picked up on that.)

Rejection letters are a blow to even the strongest ego, but they can teach you a few things, besides humility. They can show you where your work isn't working, where you need to concentrate your creative fire, and what you might have to do to leap that final hurdle into publication, especially when you note that the same criticisms keep coming back.

But I don't care how many times you hear about some writers who are so cool and confident that they festoon their walls with their rejection slips—I say read 'em, once, and then *throw them out*!

RULE 61.

INDULGE THE FANTASY.

One of the sticks with which aspiring writers are often hit over the head is this: "Do you want to write . . . or do you just want to be a writer?"

You're supposed to be chastened by that. Real writers, you're to understand, want to write; they *need* to write. Phonies just think about sitting around in comfy armchairs, being interviewed about what they've already written, surrounded by leather-bound collections of their work, a faithful dog, and a worshipful spouse.

To which I say, what's wrong with that? What's wrong with having a picture in your head of yourself as an accomplished and successful writer? We all have to have some goal we're striving for, some idea of what we're aiming at—and the image of yourself basking in the glory and accolades is as good as any.

What, pray tell, is the alternative?

Should you imagine yourself, day after day, year after year, toiling over a cluttered desk, or wrestling a new ink cartridge into your printer? (I know that laser printers are supposed to be much better, but this little inkjet baby, sitting to my left, has been cranking away with no problem for well over a decade. I'm patting it on the head now.) What kind of a fantasy is it to imagine penury and neglect? How is that supposed to get you excited, or keep you motivated?

No, I say go right ahead and dream away. Color in every square inch of your private fantasy. Savor every detail. No writer focuses on the image of himself writing, any more than a bus driver dreams—except in his nightmares—of driving a bus. Yes, you have to do the work, and yes, you *will* do it; that's a given. Writing—though it can be rewarding and even, on a good day, fun—is hard work, and no one would want to dwell on it overly much.

Consider this fantasizing not as a waste of mental energy but as a kind of self-actualization. (Now we're talking!) By concentrating on the end, not the means, you may be able to keep some of the troubles and doubts at bay. Thinking about your writing tends to become thinking about the *problems* in your writing. Thinking about flying first-class to collect your Nobel Prize tends to become . . . wonderful. Thinking about syntax and structure will keep you up all night, while thinking about elegant receptions and sleek black limousines will put you to sleep, with a smile on your face.

And nothing, or so I'm told, will help you write better than a good night's rest.

RULE 62.

KEEP YOUR DAY JOB.

But enjoyable as fantasizing can be—and I devote a healthy two or three hours a day to it myself—it's also important to be realistic about your writing. Especially when it comes to money.

In one of my classes, a female banker was determined to pin me down on the subject of her royalties. Even though she hadn't actually written or sold her book yet, she wanted to know how soon she could quit her job at the bank and start living off her writing income. When I explained, as I often have to do, that royalties are like quarks—"We theorize that they exist, but we never actually see them"—she was not amused. Some writers are so focused on the bottom line that they forget to pay enough attention to what they have to do first. Namely, write. (Which isn't to say, by the way, that you will never see any royalties—one day you may. Just don't plan your life around them.)

We all read in the papers about the monster deals made by writers like J. K. Rowling and Donna Tartt and James Patterson. But those deals are in the paper *because* they're such big news—and so rare. Most writers labor in obscurity, for far less money. The writers who make their fortunes the first time out of the gate are one in a million. It's all about as reliable as the slot machines in Las Vegas.

But if what you want to do is improve your chances of seeing a check in the mail, there *are* a few things you should know. One is that non-fiction sells more easily than fiction. Newspapers and magazines have a bottomless craving for news stories, features, trend pieces, profiles, travel essays, humor columns. They don't just *want* these things—they *need* them, or else they're going to have to run blank pages in between all the ads they've already sold.

Publishers want nonfiction, too. The commercial viability of a non-fiction proposal, or manuscript, is much easier for them to assess than a novel. They can gauge, with some accuracy, how big an audience exists for your book idea, and how many of these potential customers are likely to come out and buy it. If you've got a great new idea for a book about dieting, relationships, careers, then they want to hear from you.

If, on the other hand, you have a novel, they may—or may not—want to hear from you. Publishers are always looking for the next big blockbuster (or the next writer capable of churning them out), but they're also very gun shy. Most novels that they buy don't do very well, so they're reluctant to invest much time or money, particularly in newcomers. They buy warily, promote stingily, and publish with little fanfare. Collections of short stories are even harder to sell; if stories are what you're interested in writing, your best bet is to start selling them to small literary magazines and gradually build a reputation that will catch the attention of a book editor or publishing house.

One writer I know, lamenting the boom-or-bust nature of the writing life, put it nicely when he said, "You can get rich at this, but you just can't make a living."

Keep the day job until you can deposit your big, fat advance from the big, fat publishing house, in the bank—and even then, wait three days for the check to clear.

RULE 63.

PICK A PERSONAGE.

If writing is, at its most fluent, a form of talking, then the question you have to ask yourself is, *Who's doing the talking?*

It's either you, in the first person—as in "I took my leave of the gendarmes"—or it's you in some variation of the third person—as in "Raoul took his leave of the gendarmes." (It could be you in the second person, I suppose—as in "You take your leave of the gendarmes"—but to pull that off at any length, you'd have to be Jay McInerney, who made the technique famous years ago in his novel *Bright Lights, Big City*. Nearly everyone who tried it afterward (and plenty did) failed miserably.

No, it's either going to be first or third, and in both instances, of course, it's going to be you behind the curtain, doing the talking for everybody. It's your writing, and you're creating everything on the page. But have you chosen the right voice to do it in, after all?

When you're really planning to whale away, the first person is your ticket. It's the closest you'll get to your own voice. (Your writing voice is always, no matter what you do, going to be at least one shade off your spoken voice, if only because it's an edited and shaped version of the original.) In a sustained narrative, the first person solves a lot of problems for you. If "I" am telling the story, then it's only what *I* know, and *I* see, and *I* hear, that I can relate. It's easy to maintain the focus, and the intensity, of the story, and at the same time to forge an intimate bond with the reader. That's probably why a lot of antiheroes use it; it's hard for readers to hate someone who's been whispering so openly and confidingly in their ear.

But what if the first person isn't working out for you? It happens a lot, and usually it's because the material is so close to you, so personal and revealing, that the same impulse that originally drove you to write in the first person is now warning you to back off, to cool down, to conceal some things. You're growing uncomfortable with owning up to what's on the page.

And that's true even if the first-person narrator is someone else entirely, someone you've made up out of whole cloth. I don't care if you're lurking behind a character named Englebert or Brunhilda— sometimes that "I" can feel too restricting, and too close, and you can't quite shake feeling identified with it somehow. Worse, you can't help thinking that readers are going to confuse the two of you—author and character—somehow, the way they confuse actors with the roles they've played on screen. Philip Roth, who openly used his own life and experiences to enrich so many of his books, was often conflated with some of the less than admirable characters he wrote about.

That's when you might want to think about shifting your narrative to the third person. Try writing the same pages in the third person and see if that doesn't free you up. Sometimes all you need is to change "I'd been happily married for ten years, and yet felt irresistibly drawn to this mysterious stranger," to "Alex had been happily married for ten years, and yet felt irresistibly drawn to this mysterious stranger." The first one will have your mother calling to find out what's wrong in your marriage, and the other will have the Lifetime network calling to buy the story rights.

RULE 64.

HAM IT UP.

The one place where the first-person point of view was traditionally verboten was journalism.

If you were a reporter, writing for a newspaper or magazine, you were strongly advised, if not downright forbidden, ever to say "I," or to refer to yourself in the story. If you had to, it was under such strange locutions as "this reporter," or the editorial "we," for which the *New Yorker* "Talk of the Town" pieces were so well-known—and so often mocked. ("We were delighted to attend the Pointillist exhibition at the Academy of the Arts, where we enjoyed cucumber sandwiches cut to precisely the right size.")

And in some quarters, little has changed. If you're writing for the front page of the *New York Times*, you are probably going to be limited to official, third-person journalese, and the only indication that you personally are doing the reporting will be your byline at the top of the story. But guess what? If it's the *New York Times*, that's plenty!

But in many other quarters, things have gotten a lot looser. With the advent of what is called everything from "creative journalism" to "literary nonfiction" to the "literature of fact," writers have been allowed, if not encouraged, to sneak themselves into the story and on camera. And yet, even though that privilege has been proffered, many writers have been loath to accept it. Either they are too timid to exploit the opportunity, or too confined by previous expectations and long-standing rules to take advantage of this big chance. And even when they do, they limit themselves to innocuous observations or unrevealing asides.

Sometimes the material is so lively and engaging it speaks for itself, but many times it's not—and that's when a bold, opinionated, authorial voice can save the day. Many times, all a piece of nonfiction writing needs to jazz it up is a loud strong intrusion from the writer! What were your personal feelings about your subject? What surprised you, bothered you, pleased you—*personally*? Was the staff at the ultra-fabulous resort you'd booked a room at too ultra-fabulous to get the right bags to your room? Or, did you perhaps have some unusual interaction with one of the people you were writing about in a piece? Did a famous athlete, whom you thought illiterate, share with you a tour of his rare book collection? Did you catch a prima ballerina gobbling down a bag of pork rinds? Did the nuclear physicist want nothing more than to play a video game with you? By putting yourself into the story—not necessarily at its center, but there, present and accounted for, nonetheless—you can add zest and color and, above all, immediacy, to even the driest of topics (and maybe even get a sprinkling of stardust on your own shoulders).

RULE 65.

KNOW NO SHAME.

Of the many privileges afforded a writer, perhaps the one I cherish most is the right to be nosy.

If you're a writer, you get to ask anybody just about anything. You get to pull out your pad (you are carrying one now, right?) and fire away at anyone. "What first got you interested in building an atomic reactor in your yard? How exactly do you find your fissionable material? Is your wife an enthusiast, too?" Although, in a case like this, your next call might be to the FBI, in most such instances you'll be dialing up an editor, to pitch the fascinating story you've just stumbled across.

Writers are not only entitled to be inquisitive, they're required to be. If you're not interested in what the people around you are doing, and why they're doing it, then you're probably not destined to write for newspapers or magazines. In fact, you're probably not suited to writing fiction, either, because what makes most fiction work is its characters. Aside from certain best sellers that, to my mind, have only cardboard characters being put through their assigned paces by an author more interested in plot than people (I mention no names), good novels and short stories are populated by characters whose complex personalities and motivations drive the story, and make the book impossible to put down.

Take *Atonement*, the well-known novel by Ian McEwan (also turned into an Academy Award–winning movie starring Keira Knightley and Saoirse Ronan). In the first half of the book, almost nothing happens. Really. An aristocratic family assembles at a country house, a letter is misdelivered, and an impressionable girl sees some things she's too young to understand. But from just such quotidian stuff, a story of immense drama and portent has been fashioned. And it's all because the author has, plainly, studied people, how they conduct themselves and why they do what they do.

In the best sense of the words, if there is one, McEwan is both a voyeur and an eavesdropper—and an expert one at that.

Writers have to be a bit of both. They have to understand the nuances, the elisions, the confessions and confusions that make life the unpredictable mess that it is. They must grow to observe with fastidious attention the subtle signals with which people communicate their desires and their needs, and listen, with equal care, to the way they express, or avoid, those same longings. When interviewing someone, you have to be as alive to their expressions, their gestures, their general deportment, as you are to the words your tape recorder (I always use one) is capturing. It's only when you put the two together that you get, and can give, the full picture.

To write well, about anything, you must have curiosity in your nature. To write well about people, or characters, you have to be downright shameless.

RULE 66.

PASS THE
SCUTTLEBUTT.

And while we're cultivating the negative virtues, another thing that writers should be is gossips.

There is no greater source of information in this world—easily surpassing the Library of Congress, the Encyclopedia Britannica and the internet, combined—than simple, old-fashioned, "you're not going to believe this!" gossip.

Gossip is the way we learn all the really important stuff. It's how we learn who's sleeping with whom, who's making more money than we are, who our true friends and secret enemies are. Gossip is a kind of interpersonal barter, a money-less exchange where we get to trade nuggets of information. *I'll tell you what went down after the party ended if you tell me why Cindy won't look me in the eye anymore.* To get the good stuff in return, you have to have something to give up; otherwise, people stop trading with you. Good gossip is valuable, and everybody expects a quid pro quo.

As a writer, you want to be sure to have a ready stock on hand; that way, you'll always be able to pick up more. But why do you want it? That's easy. You want it because gossip is the unofficial version of events, it's the private face of public affairs. Gossip fills in all the gaps, explains all the motivations, charts all the currents. It's the common coin of human commerce, and no writer can ever have enough of it.

Whether you're trying to create complex characters for a story, or write a nuanced profile of a public figure, you're going to have to rely on what you know of human nature, what you've come to understand about how we all really behave and why we do the things we do. The official account seldom covers that. We learn about people from other people, from talking to them, swapping stories and opinions, jokes and observations.

We also learn about ourselves; one of the greatest virtues of gossip is that it gives us a chance—in a casual, nonjudgmental format—to check our own proclivities and attitudes against everybody else's. *Is it wrong to make out in the supply closet? Do other people chisel a bad waiter on the tip? Does anyone else forget his parents' birthdays?* As writers, we're always trying to figure out if we're crazy or not (generally, the answer is yes) but gossip is a good way to keep track.

RULE 67.

COME TO YOUR SENSES.

Most writers lean on their visual sense first and foremost. They see the scene unfolding before their eyes—the car chase, the regatta, the dinner party—or else the character taking physical shape. Is she tall and lean, in jeans and a parka, or old and infirm, stooped over and wrapped in a threadbare shawl? Our eyes reap and transmit most of the sensory information available to us.

But let's not forget all those other useful senses that we regularly employ.

Auditory, for instance. What do your characters sound like? Think not only of how they speak—grammatically? coarsely? beguilingly? with a foreign accent?—but of their tone and volume. And are there other noises going on in your scene—the clatter of a busy restaurant kitchen, the rumble of a factory line, the buzzing of bumblebees in a garden? The sounds of your scene really help to bring it home to readers in a visceral way.

So do the smells, though they are famously hard to describe. How do you describe the unmistakable scent of salt water without saying it smelled like ocean water with salt in it? But olfactory cues are some of the strongest we have. Think of how you are transported by the aroma of freshly baked cookies or the mouthwatering scent of a steak grilling on your neighbor's backyard barbecue? To this day I can't smell cinnamon without thinking of my mom's French toast, which was liberally sprinkled with it.

Taste is tough, too, though Marcel Proust had only to take a bite of the madeleine to be transported into another time and place, and come out on the other end with the masterwork, *Remembrance of Things Past*, seven volumes long. (I confess to only plowing through two of them, but even the truncated journey was memorable.)

Tactile sensations aren't to be overlooked, either. *Story of O,* for instance, is a famously erotic tale, and I was given a copy as a gift by an old girlfriend. (Still not sure what message she was trying to send, since, as I recall, she broke up with me a week later.) Anyway, I read it, and apart from all the wildly improbable S&M sex, the book was one of the most sensual stories I had ever read. No garment went undescribed, no bedroom, no dungeon cell. The author, Anne Desclos, writing under the pseudonym Pauline Réage, wasn't only paying attention to the contortions of the characters—and man, did they get up to outlandish stuff—but she was coloring in every scene with intimate physical sensations having to do with touch and scent and sound. You could feel the swish of the dresses that the women were wearing (or doffing), the smell of their various perfumes, and I'm convinced that it was her ability to conjure up these sensory elements that set the book apart from tons of other tawdrier erotica and has kept it in print since 1954.

But then again, maybe it *was* just the crazy sex . . .

RULE 68.

TURN UP THE HEAT.

Speaking of which . . . just in case you haven't heard about this, sex sells.

Yes, I know. Shocking.

But if anyone doubted it, the phenomenal success of *Fifty Shades of Grey*, ten years ago, made it plain that there was an unbounded audience for erotica. No one was more surprised by the unprecedented success of that franchise, initially self-published, than its author, E. L. James. She benefited, in large measure, from the fact that e-books were coming into their own, and women could now indulge in racy reading on an airplane or a subway without anyone being the wiser.

The effect on fiction is, I think still being felt. The gloves came off (with everything else), and novels—not just romance stuff, but mainstream books—became more graphic and unconstrained—which left me, and many another novelist, wondering just what the boundaries were now, and how far to push against them. In one novel I wrote, the editor memorably complained to me that it took three hundred pages before my hero and heroine finally went to bed, and even then I'd made the mistake of no sooner letting them slide between the sheets than I discreetly cut to the curtains blowing in the wind. "What are you thinking?" she protested. "You finally got them into bed! We want to know what happens there! Turn up the heat, don't turn off the oven."

Well, okay. I thought it was fairly obvious what went on there, but these days readers don't want to be cheated out of some erotic thrills. And if you're writing a romance novel or something expressly aimed at a female audience primed for such stuff, you had better deliver. Not cutting away at the critical moments, but also, unless you are deliberately trying to shock, no undue emphasis on the raunch factor, either.

The best sex scenes are not particularly mechanical; we all know what goes where by now. What makes sex scenes really sizzle is our emotional investment in the characters. Rather than spending your time describing the acrobatics, focus on the feelings and the perceptions of the people involved. Write the scene from inside someone's point of view, with all the thoughts that race through the head while all sorts of other stuff is going on down below. Get close to the sights and smells, the tastes and sensations, that the lover is experiencing—the specifics—and the impact will be greater than any amount of purely clinical description.

Also, choose your vocabulary carefully. There are nineteen different words for the major pieces of sexual equipment—male and female—and you have to decide just how coarse, or delicate, you want to be. Think hard about the kind of book you're writing, and who its intended audience is, before committing yourself. If, for instance, it's meant for one of the popular romance lines, read a few of those first, and from that you'll get a good idea of the proper pitch. (I remember one well-known brand had a style sheet that described exactly what sort of thing they wanted, how far the heroine should go, and what words to use in conveying the action.) When in doubt, my own feeling is, rein it in. Your readers' own imaginations can be counted on to do a lot of the heavy lifting—and breathing.

RULE 69.

GO INSIDE.

It's easy to accept the acceptable, to applaud the laudable.

But it's quite another to accept the *un*acceptable, to find in ourselves the capacity to understand, and even forgive, conduct and behavior that we regard as reprehensible or worse. For writers, that's where the going gets rough.

And interesting.

If, instead of stereotyping people, or portraying them with a few slapdash effects, we can fully imagine them, and enter into the world *as they perceive it*, then we've gone right through the looking glass and into the heart and soul of the character. If we can suspend our personal judgment and see things as they do, feel things as they feel them, then we've managed to go where we were truly meant to go.

It's one reason artists are drawn to the challenge of presenting the otherwise unpresentable, of delving into the seamy, the sordid, the morally offensive. Sure, it makes for good material—who wants to read about a bunch of upright citizens all the time?—but it also forces the writer to raise his or her game. Can you dig deep enough to find the common humanity? Can you identify, vicariously, with even the most shocking desires, and make them comprehensible to your audience? Your readers don't have to like your characters—heck, you probably don't like them all yourself—but if you've made your audience feel what it is to be inside their skin, you've done your job, and then some. For a master class, you can read Tom Perrotta's *Little Children*, with its wide cast including porn addicts, sex offenders, and everyday adulterers.

The same holds true for nonfiction. Interview one of these conspiracy nuts and it's easy as pie to make him look and sound ridiculous—but, once published, the interview is just as easily dismissed, and forgotten. What did you tell us that we didn't already know, or that your subject hadn't made clear in his own words? Nothing. But if you could drop your defenses, as it were, if you could open yourself up and simply see things through your subject's eyes, it's possible that you could come back with something truly revealing—maybe even something constructive. How did he get that way? What experiences shaped him? How have his perceptions become so hateful or skewed? Come up with answers to questions like these, and you might even keep such weeds from springing up elsewhere. Must you become some crusader on a mission? Hardly. But practicing empathy, a kind of divine omniscience and benign acceptance, can help you to get the story—and it can also help you to find the *real* story, the one lying just below. The one that shows us not just what happened—that's usually the easy part—but *why* it did.

RULE 70.

DE-CLAIM! DE-CLAIM!

At one time, if you saw somebody talking to himself on the street, it was a dead giveaway—the guy was bonkers. But now that we all carry cell phones and some of us even wear earbuds (why do those things never stay in my ears? are my ears deformed?) it's not so simple.

Which is good news for writers. One more professional tic—chattering on when there's no one else around—has become less noticeable. The social stigma is gone!

Talking to yourself is the best way, in my book, to iron out all the last stubborn wrinkles in your prose. What looks perfectly good on the page—smooth and streamlined and effortless—may not sound so good when you actually try to utter it aloud. Dialogue that you thought was clever and punchy may sound elliptical and baffling when you act it out; sometimes you may even discover that certain lines can't be said without running out of breath. And narrative passages that seemed downright poetic when you wrote them may come off as overblown, purple and pompous; if you inexplicably find yourself orating them with an English accent, then that should tell you something right there.

But you don't have to be a thespian of the first order to reap the benefits of reading aloud. All you have to do is close the door to your office (no point in alarming other members of the household) and softly, but audibly, pronounce the words you've written. Where do you stumble? Where do you momentarily lose the sense of what you're saying? Where do you find the same words recurring too often? Do you, at some point, lose the narrative thread of your own prose?

The thing to keep in mind is, all writing is written to be heard, even if that means in absolute silence, under the nose of the scariest librarian. You're asking your readers to *hear* the words in their own heads, and respond to them accordingly. You're asking that same reader, if your work includes quotations or speaking parts, to assume those roles and listen to those lines, too, as you have written them. Because of your extraordinary skills as a writer, you've provided a lot of clues, in the specific words you've chosen and in the artful way you have chosen to deploy them. But if the words don't ring true when you try them out, then they will surely sound false in the more strictly enforced privacy of a reader's skull.

RULE 71.

TAKE THE LONG WAY.

Speaking of a reader's skull, let me just say that there's a lot more room in there than you might imagine.

We all hear a lot these days about the shrinking attention span of the American public. Corrupted by Twitter, TV commercials, movie trailers, computer games, and music videos where the images stream by at the speed of light, we are all supposedly incapable of holding a thought for more than a minute without impatiently switching to something else.

And yet, books that weigh a ton keep right on selling. Stephen King, Anne Rice, Hilary Mantel, Dan Brown—none of them can be accused of going light on the keyboard. Historical tomes and hefty biographies, from fine writers like David McCullough, Walter Isaacson, and Niall Ferguson, never fail to find an enthusiastic reception. And whether or not you think these books could actually *use* a bit of judicious pruning, they are clearly satisfying a large audience just the way they are.

Nothing encourages me more.

Readers, or at least an awful lot of them, are still embracing full-bodied books, books that don't stint on anything. Novels with large casts of characters and complex plots that cover long spans of time, stories that traverse whole continents or even galaxies. That's what books can do, like nothing else can. A huge special effect in a book costs no more, in ink and paper, than does the smallest observation. And people are still turning to them for just that reason.

Writers, as a result, need never hold back. If in your novel you want to flash back to your heroine's youth, and show some incidents from her formative years, go right ahead—and if you want to stay there for a hundred pages, feel free. True, you have to make that material interesting, and I'm not saying your book should be padded, *but* you don't have to hold back because you think your readers may not be able to handle it. They can handle anything you throw at them, and truth be told, many readers (and I'd have to number myself among them) enjoy a big, fat wallow. When I choose a book to read, I am also choosing a world in which I plan to immerse myself for some time. It's one reason I don't cotton so much to short stories—reading a short story makes me feel like I just got wet and already I have to get out of the bath. A big book is like an Olympic-sized pool, and once I'm in, lying on my raft with a cool drink in hand, I want to hang out for days on end.

Whether it's a political biography or a multigenerational saga, let your narrative unfold in as lush and deliberate a manner as you choose. If it's interesting to you, then there's a very good chance it will be interesting to others, too. Who would have thought that the story of a long-forgotten racehorse, told in over for four hundred pages, would grip millions of readers? I doubt that even Laura Hillenbrand, who wrote *Seabiscuit*, had expectations that high. But breakout books like that just go to show you: readers—good ones—are willing to follow the right writer, telling the right story, to the race track, or pretty much anywhere.

RULE 72.

SHOW NO MERCY.

At my first magazine job in New York, my boss kept telling me, "Writers don't write, they *rewrite*."

Every time I heard it, I wanted to weep.

And I didn't believe it. Every time I did have to rewrite something, I took it as a sign that I wasn't really very good at this, and that I should start looking for a more suitable line of work at my earliest opportunity.

To be perfectly frank, I still think that what flows from my keyboard should be so pristine that it allows for no further improvement . . . and to this day I'm perplexed that it's not. But at least, in a small sign of progress, I *do* accept the fact that it's not.

Writing is a process—of discovery, of refinement, of invention. The notion that you can just bang it out in immaculate condition is worse than arrogant—it's positively self-destructive. First of all, you'll give yourself a complex, trying to write perfect prose all the time, and thinking that all the other writers out there are somehow pulling it off. Second, you'll fail to do what needs to be done to make your work as good as it could, and should, be.

William Faulkner, in an oft-quoted remark, said "You've got to kill all your darlings," and while I think that may be a bit of an overstatement—surely *some* of your darlings can be spared—I take his general point. You have to be ruthless, in the service of the work. Many times the very thing that sparked your imagination, that got you writing this particular piece in the first place, will turn out to be, by the time you're done, irrelevant, or beside the point. There's even a chance that it will have been superseded by something better, more apposite, which only occurred to you while writing. Most good things occur to you not while you're *thinking* about writing, but while you're actually doing it. This is something that legions of would-be writers never grasp; they claim that they've composed entire stories, novels, scripts, but that so far, they just haven't found the time to get them down on paper. Tapping their foreheads with one finger, they say, with a wink,

"It's all right up here." Which is where, nine times out of ten, it is very likely to remain.

Great writing is seldom simply accomplished in one fell swoop—and if you still don't believe me, check out the manuscript pages of any famous writer's work, and you will see the welter of corrections, elisions, emendations, that occurred before the final work went out into the world. You'll see so many squiggles and cross-outs and arrows pointing to revisions scribbled in the margin that it can be hard to decipher the remaining words below. There's an old saw that says no one should ever watch laws or sausages being made, but the same, I'm afraid, goes for most great prose.

DOUBT EVERYONE.

Writing can be a lonely task, and one way that a lot of writers have gotten around that problem—particularly, as I've mentioned, in Hollywood, where comedy teams proliferate—is by becoming a team. Having somebody else in the room with you, particularly when it comes to trying out comedic banter, is a big help. If you can't get your partner to laugh, it's back to the drawing board.

In the greater world, many writers turn to local writing groups, where several writers get together every week, or maybe every month, to share their work and offer critiques and encouragement. Some of these groups even specialize—one might be for mystery writers, another for memoirists, etc. And while I think the encouragement part is nice—helpful and soul-sustaining—there is also a risky downside.

Whenever your work comes out for a public airing, it runs the risk of getting diluted. Everybody in the writing group is going to have an opinion, and while some of these comments might be useful and on point, others won't be. Will you always be able to distinguish between them? Especially when you are in the middle of composition? What if somebody had told Beethoven that starting the Fifth Symphony with several straight D flats was boring? What if somebody told Michelangelo that painting a ceiling was a bad idea—"who ever looks up there?"—but that the floor, now that was something to think about! What if someone had told Victor Hugo his ending for *The Hunchback of Notre Dame* was too downbeat, and why *couldn't* Quasimodo and Esmeralda just find a way to make it work together?

Even the most well-intentioned advice can be distracting, if not destructive. I have personally witnessed fresh and original work get mauled in a group discussion, and seen the writer leave with the impression that she should come up with something more predictable and in keeping with the group consensus. It's easy to be swayed, especially if more than one person is clamoring in your ear. I mean, who

among us is 100 percent confident about every single thing in the work
at hand?

Democracy is fine when it comes to government, but in the arts it
is awfully fallible. What does the public know? Sometimes, nothing.
Van Gogh couldn't sell his paintings, Manet was reviled by the academy, Melville starved, Stravinsky's *The Rite of Spring* was booed, John
Kennedy Toole couldn't get *A Confederacy of Dunces* published until
he was dead, J. P. Donleavy's *The Ginger Man* was rejected dozens of
times, even though it has since been voted one of the 100 best books of
the last century. J. K. Rowling had a devil of a time placing her first
Harry Potter book. I could go on for days.

And don't even get me started on editors and agents. Because of
their professional status, their opinions take on extra weight. I had one
agent who routinely vetoed my nonfiction book ideas, telling me they
were "articles, not books." And I believed him, until I started noticing
that six months to a year later, these very same ideas were showing up
as other people's books. I may have been behind the curve a bit, but
I was *not* completely out to lunch. Magazine editors, too, have often
taken a pass on feature ideas I pitched to them, and that later turned
up elsewhere, in some very similar incarnation. I'm not blaming them,
they're only human—but I am saying that even these professionals
don't always *know*.

If you're going to listen to other people's opinions—whether it's by
joining a writing group, consulting with an agent, or pitching to an
editor—proceed with caution. Remember at all times that there is only
one opinion that matters in the end—and that's yours.

RULE 74.

FIND YOUR IDEAL.

For those who don't wish to keep their writing under close wraps, hermetically sealed until ready for immediate publication, there is a compromise solution.

And that would be your ideal reader.

Although writing groups can prove dangerous, so can writing in total secrecy. You may be a writer who *needs* to check in with the world now and then, and have some validation of the work you're doing. You may *want* to have the occasional course corrective, or constructive (if you can find it) criticism. You may need to air your prose and get some idea of how the world will react to the finished work. And for that, you need a sounding board.

Which is easier said than found.

You need to find someone at least as intelligent as yourself (and Lord *knows* how hard that is!). But wedded to this intelligence must be an innate sense of diplomacy. Your reader must be a good enough friend to tell you the truth, but so sensitive to your moods and attitude that the truth is delivered in a safe, benign, and tactful manner. Already we're approaching the realm of the impossible.

Should your ideal reader be a writer him or herself? On the one hand, a fellow scribe may be better at pinpointing the problems in your work, and possible solutions; you can really talk craft, nuts and bolts stuff, with someone who's wrestled with those same issues.

But on the other hand, a civilian can give you the kind of John Q. Public reaction that generally matters the most. What will the everyday reader make of your work? Will it find an audience in the great beyond?

The decision is up to you. For years, my own ideal reader was another writer, Linda, who lived exactly equidistant from a Greek diner called the Silver Star, which was open twenty-four hours a day, and always busy (their rice pudding with cinnamon and whipped cream was the best). There we could get together, often late at night, with menus as stiff and unwieldy as Parcheesi boards, to offer each other advice and counsel (though she was a bit older, and way more successful, than I was, and as a result had a lot more worthwhile things to say).

But oddly enough, even though I now live three thousand miles away from Linda, and we talk no more than every other month, she is still in some sense my ideal reader. When I write something funny, I find myself thinking, "Would Linda laugh?" When I'm writing something sober, I think, "Would Linda approve?" Or would she highlight—oh so gently—some problem I hadn't seen? Whether physically present, marking up your manuscript, or spiritually hovering, whispering suggestions in your ear, your ideal reader is the one, deep inside yourself, whom you would most like to wow. And if that ideal reader keeps saying this or that passage needs just one more rewrite or tweak, pay attention. Chances are, she's onto something.

RULE 75.

KILL THE PASSION.

Your blood is boiling. Your dander is up. You can hardly wait to start writing. In fact, you're not going to wait another second! You're going to sit down and scrawl the electric words, the timeless thoughts, that are coursing through your veins like fire—*God, doesn't it feel good to get it all out!*—before you lose an ounce of the passion you're feeling right now. Isn't that what all the writing books and instructors are always telling you to do—write out of passion?

Be my guest—write out of all the passion you can manage, write while your hair is frizzing with feeling, while your skin is tingling. Write away, with fervor and abandon—but just understand that it won't be letter perfect, or even close to it, when you're done.

Passion—whether it's anger or indignation, love or lust, hatred or sorrow—is wonderful fuel, burning hot and burning bright, but it's also burning out of control. When you're in the throes of these emotions, you're not thinking all that clearly, and you're probably not writing that way, either. You're pouring it all out on the page, raw, unrefined, unmediated and un-meditated upon. It's like going on a crying jag—cathartic, draining, and ultimately a relief. For you.

But not necessarily for the reader.

Passion has a way of clouding the judgment (ever fall madly in love with somebody who wasn't really right for you?) and it has a way of muddying up prose, too. The immortal Oscar Wilde wrote a deeply passionate prison letter, *De Profundis*, to his erstwhile lover, Lord Alfred Douglas, but even he went on and on, around and around in circles, mixing up all kinds of clever insights and fine turns of phrase (he wasn't Oscar Wilde for nothing!) with vast swaths of bathos and repetitive twaddle. (Of course, it didn't help the poor guy that his jailers limited not only his time but his access to paper; each page was often confiscated before he could move on to the next.) But more to the point, for all his self-flagellation, Wilde went right back to his toxic lover as soon as he was released—which just goes to show that even genius can't see straight when passion enters the picture.

What you feel strongly, and strongly about, is of course great material from which to mine your future work—and write it all down, as you feel it, as freely as you like. But regard it as the ore, not the finished work into which it must be transmuted. Even a newspaper editorial, written with all the heat and haste that you felt overwhelming you in the act of composition, needs to cool off overnight. The next day you'll be surprised to see that, for all its energy, it's not perhaps as persuasive, or even as coherent, as it could be. It may seem—even to you, its author—intemperate or convoluted. (So you can only imagine how it would strike the average reader.) By and large, writing with a little less passion, and a little more polish, serves everyone a lot better. Even the best-baked pie needs to cool off on the windowsill for a bit.

RULE 76.

GRUMBLE AND FUSS.

Years ago, I was at a dinner party in Chicago where one of the other guests, a local author, leaned back in his chair and declared, "I've never written a word that I'm not proud of." A general silence fell, followed by the obligatory murmur of appreciation. What else could you do?

And I suppose you could say that it's *nice* he was proud of every word he's ever written; after all, who would want to be ashamed of his or her own work? Who would want to have to deny it in public—"That rubbish, with *my* name on it? Must be a mistake—I never saw the stuff in my life."

But at the same time, it made me suspicious then, and it makes me suspicious now. I don't really know many satisfied writers—in fact, apart from that guy, I don't think I know any—and that seems to me to be about right. Writers *should* be unsatisfied with their work. It's part of our job description.

Writers tend to be obsessive creatures; we live much of the time in our own heads, where we make the rules and where we have only illusory playmates to join in the planned activities. And if any of them misbehaves, they can be banished, instantly. Writers are born autocrats.

But we are also our own worst enemies. Every sentence, every word, every syllable sometimes, gets the once-over, more than once, and what seems fine to us today looks wretched to us tomorrow.

And sometimes appalls us when it's finally in print.

Most writers, reading their own work, seldom see all the good stuff, and when they do, they usually gloss over it. What they see instead are the passages that rattle badly, the paragraphs that begin with a whimper, the humorous asides that fall flat. They hear the verbal echoes that they can't believe they didn't hear before, they see the gaps where a necessary connection should have been made, the fine flourishes that look more like silly frippery now.

Like actors who claim to hate watching themselves on screen, writers often hate to read their own work. (But we mean it.) Oblivious to the merits, alert to the faults, we find it less than an enjoyable experience. But that inveterate dissatisfaction is what marks us as writers in the first place. If you want to write, you want to get it right—you worry over every word. And that worry—sorry to say—never really goes away. Every time something you wrote appears—in the newspaper, between book covers, on the movie screen—you will want to call out, "Hold it!" Why? Because you've just had a better idea; you've just seen a way to do it just a little bit differently, just a little bit better.

But don't fret. Cherish your malcontent status, and remember: The best writers are always striving, however impossibly, for perfection.

RULE 77.

ENGAGE THE ENEMY.

Don't let anybody kid you—both successful writers and unsuccessful writers procrastinate; it's as common as a computer glitch, and just as unnerving. But there is one big difference.

Successful writers get over it.

One of my best buddies in college was a guy we called Greenie—brilliant fellow, terrific writer (when he could be made to). But there was just something about an assignment and its deadline that made Greenie put on the brakes. If a paper was due on a Tuesday, he couldn't be made to start it any time sooner than the Wednesday after. While all the rest of us were grinding away on our theses—a yearlong project, necessary for graduation—Greenie was reading Sainte-Beuve, in French, for fun, and arguing about philosophy over endless cups of coffee in the student center.

During one of these conversations, Greenie asked me, in all seriousness, how I did it—how I kept my nose to the grindstone and actually arranged to turn things in when they were due. "I mean," he said, in a spirit of inquiry and not admiration, "how do you do it?"

Hmm. I had to think about it, but eventually I came up with a multipart answer. For one thing, I did it because I was, and still am, compulsive by nature. And competitive—I wanted to get that A in the course. I also fear censure and dread authority. A coward by nature, I weep at a scornful glance.

But the real reason was more calculated than any of that, and it's just something I'd learned long before. If I put off writing a school paper until it was almost due, the leisure time, I discovered, wasn't really all that leisurely. I'd walk around feeling guilty and beleaguered, with a sense of pressure building up over my head like a massive thunderstorm. This pressure only *de*creased, in an almost uncanny proportion, as the time I devoted to the work that was due *in*creased. In other words, the sooner I got down to work, the sooner the pressure let up. And the more I worked, the more that cloud hanging over my head dissipated. The calculation was a fairly simple one to make, and I never forgot it.

Procrastination doesn't make the task any sweeter or better; it just drags the whole thing out. Every day you delay makes the work look more formidable, while every day you chip away at it, even with only a few paragraphs, makes it look that much more manageable. Although I was never able to convince Greenie of this, wrestling the beast to the ground was, in the end, preferable to tiptoeing around it for weeks.

RULE 78.

MIX IT UP.

I know it's increasingly rare these days, but did you ever take a train trip, where you settled down into your seat, with a good book in your lap, and the wheels of the train rattling over the tracks, *clickety-clack, clickety-clack* . . . only to wake up hours later when the conductor shook you awake at your destination?

What lulled you into sleep wasn't the book, I hope. It was the gentle rocking of the cabin, the monotonous rhythm of the train barreling along at a steady clip, over the evenly spaced tracks, the soothing and regular predictability of it all.

But what you might enjoy in a railroad excursion is death when it comes to prose. You shouldn't fall asleep reading it, and you definitely shouldn't fall asleep writing it.

In your work, you want to shake things up. You want to follow short sentences with long ones, florid passages with more straightforward stuff, action sequences with calmer bits, love scenes with explosions (literal or otherwise). The course of your narrative, like that of true love, should not run smooth. You want your train to screech along a hairpin turn now and then, to plunge into a black tunnel, to race along an open stretch of land, then slow to climb a long ascent . . . before tearing back down again into a green valley. Think Disneyland, not Amtrak.

How can you tell when your prose needs more variety? Well, first of all, if it's putting you to sleep, it's sure to put others to sleep as well. Give it the old audio test by reading it out loud. Hearing the words spoken is the easiest way to gauge their effect. Notice, in particular, if your breathing remains perfectly regular. Are you able to recite the lines with a predictable beat? Do you, in fact, sort of know, at all times, just what's coming next? Is everything laid out as perfectly as a topiary garden? Are there no abrupt switches in rhythm? No changes from humor to pathos, from bold statement to subtle insinuation, from the matter-of-fact to the sublime? From straightforward narrative to rat-a-tat dialogue?

Any time you hear yourself falling into a singsong rhythm, much less stifling a yawn, you know that things need a little pick-me-up, an alteration in tone or mood, or simply a change of scene. Imagine yourself at the throttle of the train, gazing out at the tracks ahead— is everything straight and level? Then imagine, just for the sake of variety, what else you might see out there. How might you wake up your snoozing passengers? By pulling back on the brakes? Pushing forward on the throttle? Or, at the very least, giving one long, loud, eardrum-shattering blast on the whistle?

RULE 79.

GRAPH IT.

Ever notice how magazines break up dense blocks of text with what is called in the business a "pull-quote"? That's a quote from the article, reprinted in larger type than the rest, and giving the page, which would otherwise be nothing but unalleviated copy, a less forbidding appearance. The reader needs an occasional break, or oasis, for both his eye and his mind.

The same goes when you're writing your own deathless prose. If all you see on the page is a block of words, with no indentations, no dialogue, no line breaks or subheads, you might want to look at the page again. Is it, really, all one thought? Is it all a single idea, one that does not allow for any natural pause or interruption?

Maybe it is. Maybe you are channeling, for our age, the spirit of the master of verbosity, Henry James, and your book is destined, like so many of his, to become a classic. What do I know?

But in most instances, that one super-long paragraph you've got going is actually three or four paragraphs that have been shackled together like prisoners on a chain gang and are dragging each other along. And perhaps it's time to break the chain.

A nice little paragraph indentation is like an invitation to the reader to take a breath, to blink, to stop for a second to absorb the information that just preceded it, before starting in on the great new material to come. It also suggests that you have an order to your argument, or a design to your story. A great big lump of prose looks—fairly or not— undigested, while a paragraph structure looks deliberate and carefully planned. Maybe that's why Sue Williams, a friend of mine who's a Harvard-educated lawyer (so she must know a thing or two), tells me she was taught never to write a legal brief in which a sentence was more than two lines long, or a page where there weren't at least three paragraphs. While, normally, I would never look to lawyers for advice on any kind of writing (I can't even understand the instructions on my jury summons), this strikes me as wise counsel.

Of course, *what* you're writing will also play a big part. If you're an assistant professor writing an academic paper, your paragraphs are probably going to be thicker and longer than they would if a question of tenure were not hanging in the balance; universities prize impenetrable prose. (I once tried to read a pamphlet produced by the prof in charge of the writing program [!] at a college where I was teaching, and found myself slack-jawed at its sheer incomprehensibility To think that students were supposed to learn from, and even emulate, this kind of performance made me want to guzzle an entire bottle of vodka and then hit myself over the head with the empty.)

But if you're writing a thriller, well, what could be more thrilling than pages that virtually turn themselves, where the story rushes down, in short paragraphs and simple sentences, like an avalanche gathering steam? The last chapters of my own thrillers always seem to come in quicker, punchier rhythms.

And if you're writing a comedic piece, what could be better than an abrupt halt now and then to deliver the punch line?

Newspaper stories, almost by definition, have a lot of short paragraphs; readers, it is understood, may be jouncing along in a subway car, trying to focus on a cellphone screen, or even combing over the story the old-fashioned way, with a paper spread out on a busy breakfast table. The reporter's got to make his points and then get out of the way before you turn to the next story or the Pop Tarts pop up.

RULE 80.

JOIN UP.

And now I'd like to make a point.

It's perfectly okay to start a sentence, as above, with "And."

But you were taught never to do that?

Then you were probably taught that you can't start a sentence with "But," either.

And that's untrue, too.

I've been doing both for years, ever since I started writing professionally and I was no longer in any danger of having an English teacher mark me down for it. (With only one exception, no editor—at a newspaper, magazine, or publishing house that I was working with—has ever had a problem with it.) For me, both of these ways of starting a sentence always passed the natural speech test; that is, people naturally began their sentences with both conjunctions, and if it sounded perfectly okay to my ear, and made perfect sense to the other person, then it was good enough to be written that way, too.

For me, that's always been the bottom line—does it sound right and communicate my meaning?

Writing is hard enough when you consider all the worthwhile rules that *are* worth observing. It becomes well nigh impossible when you have to worry about rules that exist simply because they've always *been* rules. And making your prose look—and sound—seamless, means, among other things, using any conjunction you need, whenever you need it. You want your sentences to flow, to meld into one another, to carry the reader along on an irresistible tide of narrative suspense, descriptive bravura, or rigorous logic. Sometimes the words and thoughts just connect effortlessly, segueing from one to another like a relay team passing the baton.

But at other times, you're going to need a conjunction, like a traffic cop, to signal the way ahead. When you say "Of course," you're usually about to make a sharp turn, as in "Of course, there are some politicians whose reputations are spotless." When you say "Furthermore," you're indicating that, to your mind, you've nailed down that last point and you're moving on to the next. When you say "Consequently," you're clearly claiming that what you're about to say proceeds incontestably from what you just said. Use these conjunctions wisely, and your readers will relax and go with the flow. Like tourists on a jumbo jet, they'll trust you to pilot the plane and keep them safe and (relatively) comfortable until they reach their final destination. (As the airline stewards are always intoning. If it's not final, it's not your destination, right?)

RULE 81.

STAKE YOUR CLAIM.

I hate moving, but I love exploring my new neighborhood. I love taking a walk down unfamiliar blocks, thinking, "Why would anyone paint a house that color?" or "Whose idea was it to put in a cactus garden in front of a Tudor cottage?" And though I think I'll never get bored with these blocks, I inevitably do.

Within a few weeks, they become nothing more than the blocks I walk the dog down.

And if I had to write about them, it'd be hard. Even though I know them well, I don't really see them any longer. I can't figure out what would make them interesting to anyone because they're no longer interesting to me. My eye has grown cold.

Sometimes, when you're writing about something terribly familiar, you have to step back and try to imagine yourself into the shoes of someone who is not familiar with it. If it's your town, or your neighborhood, try to recall what you felt when you first saw it. What surprised or delighted you? What made you decide to move there (unless it was decided for you, by the Witness Protection Program)? Now, think about how you feel when you're a tourist in a new city. You know how everything, from the pretzel carts to the statues in the park, seems new and novel and noteworthy? Well, that's how your town might look to somebody who'd never been there. That's how it once looked to you.

A new novel just came out, and it happens to take place on the campus of my alma mater—and a lot of the action occurs in the very college club of which I was a member. But what's most interesting about it to me is the way that the authors (two young guys collaborated on the book) have written about my old stomping grounds. They've managed to bring it all back to me, but at the same time show it to me in a new light. On the one hand, I'm impressed—and on the other, I'm annoyed. Strangely, it's a common writer's affliction to believe that everyplace he's been, everything's he's encountered, is territory that belongs to him alone, in perpetuity, whether he's using it for anything or not. Once in

a while, it had occurred to me to set something on that college campus—it's an idyllic spot, rich with history and Gothic buildings—but
of course I'd never gotten around to doing so. Still, how dare these
whippersnappers do it first? Have they no respect for their elders?

To make matters worse, I think these two guys have mangled certain
small but salient details about the place, mistakes that I am dying to
correct. (Since when was there a basement in the club, or a snowstorm
so late in the spring?) But to do that, I'd have to write my own book,
and that could take some time. Before somebody else comes along and
plants a flag on what by all rights should be *your* territory, stake your
claim. Immortalize your place, or your impressions, in print before a
bunch of interlopers can get their grubby mitts on it.

RULE 82.

GET IN STYLE.

When you think of most successful writers, you think first of their subject matter. Anne Rice and you think of vampires. Elmore Leonard and you think of small-time crooks and scam artists. F. Scott Fitzgerald and you conjure up the Jazz Age world of East Coast money and privilege.

But lots of writers have written about these very same subjects—there are rafts of vampire books, tons of crime capers, and no shortage of stories about rich, dissolute WASPS. So what, apart from their virtuoso storytelling, sets these writers apart, and makes their work so much more memorable than the general run?

In a word, style. You could pick up a book by any one of these writers, and without even glancing at the cover, you'd know after reading a paragraph or two whose hands you were in. Anne Rice doesn't just tell spooky stories, populated by witches and bloodsuckers; she writes in a lush, ornate style that creates a world of its own, a fever dream of sensuous detail, all evoked in a manner as indulgent and refined as some of her unforgettable characters.

Elmore Leonard captures the down-market denizens of his world in a clipped, breezy style, one that manages to indict, gently mock, and oddly coddle them, all at the same time. You root for the losers ensnared in his seemingly effortless web.

And F. Scott, my own favorite? There's a music in his prose that no one else has ever been able to capture. While there are plenty of Hemingway contests—"Write the opening of a story in Hemingway's style, and win a trip to Harry's Bar!"—there is no such thing for Fitzgerald. Why? Because his style is too subtle for that, too soft and malleable and often elegiac. It'd be like trying to imitate a flute, not a tuba. I give you, from *The Great Gatsby*: "So we beat on, boats against the current, borne back ceaselessly into the past." How can you not love that imagery, and those words?

To a great extent, you don't pick your style at all—your style picks you. And that goes just as much for an historian or biographer as it does for a novelist or short-story writer. Great historians like David McCullough or Doris Kearns Goodwin or the late Barbara Tuchman write with an inimitable and highly personal style, and even if they were to write about the very same figures or events, the accounts would wind up sounding entirely different and distinctive.

Unique as your fingerprints, your style is what enfolds your readers, what suffuses the air around them as they read, and in its many nuances conveys to them everything from mood to meaning. You've got your own style, whether you like it or not—so flaunt it.

RULE 83.

CHANGE YOUR SPOTS.

But that's not to say your style can't be, shall we say . . . calibrated.

If you could write in only one style, as sturdy and unbending as a mighty oak, you would be limiting yourself in terms of the formats you could embrace, the markets you could approach, and the audiences you could reach. Has One Size Fits All ever fit anyone well?

Let's say you like to write in a casual, colloquial style. That may work beautifully for short essays and newspaper articles, but it may not work for the big, important bildungsroman on which you feel compelled to embark. (Think hard about that decision, by the way.) Yes, you can still use your customarily graceful touch, but a style that's as light as air may not allow you the gravitas you feel your novel will require.

Conversely, you may prefer a fairly weighty delivery; maybe you're used to writing academic monographs on psycho-social problems. And now you want to switch gears for a while, and pen some whimsical piece about your daughter's first day of school. Clearly, your old scholarly style is going to pose some difficulties. "Upon arrival, the aforesaid Katie discerned a crowd of youngsters, of approximately her own age and size, but varied ethnicities, interactively engaged in rituals of acquaintanceship and familiarization, causing the subject (Katie) to respond in her immediate and predictably affective manner (i.e. crying)." Enough said. Your style has to be adjusted to fit your subject matter—and your target audience.

Which is why a working writer has to change his color as often as a chameleon. (See Rule 90 for the weariness of animal similes.) No, you can't be what you're not—a scholar can't turn himself into a comedian overnight—but you can modify your voice so that it's accommodated to its surroundings. For instance, the very last thing I do before writing a magazine, or website, piece is this: I read the publication that I'm planning to write for. If I'm writing what I hope is an op-ed piece for the *Los Angeles Times,* I scan that paper's editorial page. If I'm writing for *Cosmopolitan*, I read *Cosmopolitan* (though not in a public place).

In other words, I dip myself into the pool I hope to swim in. I get used to the feel of it, I take its temperature, so that my own writing—even though it still carries, inevitably, some of my own distinctive style—will be similar enough to fit in. David Sedaris's mordant wit might work fine for the *New Yorker*, but not so well for *Biker Babes Quarterly*.

Most writers know enough, instinctively, to do that. It comes from switching back and forth from one project to another, and from one market to another. And far from being debilitating, it's really kind of enjoyable. Instead of turning out the same old stuff, in the same old style, it gives you a chance, and a challenge, to try something new. You wind up finding new colors in your palette. When your writing starts to feel too formulaic even to you, consider a trip to some foreign creative locale—a venue you've never approached, or a form you've never attempted. Try writing a short story when you've been doing nothing but articles, for instance, or a song lyric when you've been churning out exclusively straight prose. It's like going to the gym and working out a muscle you didn't even know you had. In the end, you get what everyone wants—a more uniformly toned and attractive body (of work).

RULE 84.

TONE IT UP.

If style is the symphony, then tone is the conductor.

Just as a conductor shapes the music to his own attitude and inclinations, so your tone dictates the thrust and the import of your own work. And your tone, the way you perceive the world you're writing about—the subject you're investigating, the characters you've created, the ideas you're exploring—tells your readers how they, too, are supposed to come away feeling. Do you feel the scorn of a Voltaire . . . or the all-embracing love of a Kahlil Gibran? Are you amused, bemused, or utterly unamused? Are you sitting in judgment, or just sitting?

Tone is like the dark matter of the universe—it's everywhere, but you can't ever see it. It's there in every word choice you make—look at the difference between saying someone "waited" and someone "loitered" at the theater entrance. In the first, I'd say you were neutral; in the second, I'd say you were unfavorably disposed. And if you said that someone was "lurking" there, I'd say you were ready to call the cops.

Same event, almost the same sentence, but three very different tones, and all based on the selection of one little word. Multiply that a thousand-fold, and you see how tone pervades everything.

Writers approach their work with, first, a general worldview, ranging from a Panglossian "this is the best of all possible worlds" to "we are born into a meaningless void and die there alone" (this last author should probably seek counseling). And they also have a more *specific* attitude, one that's geared to the particular job at hand. Maybe it's an editorial on the #MeToo movement, and the writer wants to convey her own history of abuse and sexual harassment from bad bosses. Well, the tone of that piece virtually dictates itself—indignation and righteous anger, served cold for optimal flavor.

If it's some kind of fiction, your tone gets more subtly expressed, in the way, for instance, that you describe the world your characters inhabit. Like a modern-day Chekov, the Nobel-prize winning author Alice Munro writes short stories about the ordinary lives of the people in her own neck-of-the-woods—chilly Ontario, Canada—but moves backwards and forwards in time to convey, with little fanfare and much ambiguity, the poignancy of their uncelebrated trials and triumphs. Evelyn Waugh, on the other hand, had a wry contempt and derisory sense of humor, and pinned his subjects like butterflies, some still wriggling, to the walls of Oxford, Mayfair, and Brideshead. Jane Austen took the tone of a detached observer, but one to whom asperity and insight were unavoidable. Reading the work of these authors, you come away with not just a story, but a perspective, a version of reality (whatever *reality* is) slanted according to each author's lights.

In your own work, all you can do is be conscious of how your own prejudices, inclinations, and ideas are influencing your tone . . . and then judge for yourself if you're using a sledgehammer when a ball-peen hammer would do the trick, or if your tone is inviting complicity with the reader or stimulating unwanted opposition. Any tone is allowed—that's entirely your call—but the right one is often as hard to hit as a carpet tack in the dark.

RULE 85.

MAKE 'EM LAUGH!

Ever tell a joke that fell flat, and then wind up having to explain why it's funny? Humiliating.

Well, the only thing more perilous than that is encouraging people who may not have a funny bone in their bodies to try injecting some humor into their work.

But here goes, anyway.

When I say that humor is a great addition to almost any piece, I mean humor that's actually, well . . . funny. Words so amusing that they will bring out a laugh, or at least a smile. Lines that someone might want to call up a friend and quote over the phone. A turn of phrase, or a witty remark, something that surprises your readers and catches them off guard, the way that a good punch line does.

If you can come up with such stuff, you are among the blessed. (And you should quickly come out to Los Angeles, where you can get filthy rich writing jokes for network sitcoms. God knows they could use the help.) Humor is that intangible, ineffable thing that can make even the most unpalatable gruel go down; it's the leavening agent that can lighten up even the heaviest material. In fact, the heavier the material, the more an occasional touch of levity is needed; if you can find the element of the absurd, or the note of what's called "black humor," in subjects that are otherwise bleak, dreary, or depressing, you'll have gone a very long way toward engaging your readers and helping them through.

The reason I'm hemming and hawing a bit here is because I've already seen way too many books and articles that claim they can teach "anyone—and we mean anyone—to be funny!" They've actually reduced jokes and humor to weird formulae—"Set up your subject, then seek to deflate it by invoking its opposite" (huh?)—or by invoking lists of words that are, supposedly, just plain funny all the time. I'm not lying when I say that I once read a piece recommending you turn to "pickle" as the fail-safe funny word. Plug it into virtually any sentence or context and it's guaranteed to provoke a "laff riot."

Some people, as you've no doubt noticed by now, are funny by nature; it's something to do with the way they look at the world, and at themselves. Their "take" on things is somewhat askew, or off kilter. But there's just no dissecting a sense of humor; it dies on the lab table. And if it just doesn't happen to be in you, there's also no way of replicating it. That's why I've been so reluctant to insist on it. If you are funny, then be funny; your readers will love you for it. The world can always use another laugh.

But if you're not funny, that's okay, too; you don't have to be. Millions of very fine people are humor-impaired. And there's nothing more painful than watching someone straining, against all odds and personal inclinations, to be funny. It defeats the whole purpose of the exercise. "Flop sweat," as nightclub comics call it, can show up on the page just as easily as on the stage, and it'll leave your readers, like any audience, restive, uncomfortable, and signaling for the check.

RULE 86.

BEFRIEND YOUR EDITOR.

Writers can be a prickly lot, and nothing makes them pricklier than an editor.

It's just in the nature of the relationship.

Once you've gone through all the torment of writing, rewriting, and submitting something, whether it's a novel or a magazine piece, all you really want to hear (let's be honest about this) is unmitigated praise. You want the editor to snap it up, put through for immediate payment, and take you out for a fabulous, expense-account lunch.

And maybe that does happen, now and then—but it sure ain't the usual course of business. (I do remember one lunch in New York when, after I'd delivered my finished book, an editor took me out and then insisted on splitting my Boston cream pie with me. "What," I thought, "the publishing house can't afford *two* desserts?")

Once your work has been accepted for publication, you're going to hear back from an editor—and more than likely, it will be the same editor who has chosen your work in the first place. So that's a good thing—you should be predisposed to like this person, or at least to admire her taste in prose.

But she also has a job to do, and doing that job means telling you what, in her professional opinion, needs work. No matter how complimentary her remarks may be at the start, eventually they are going to move from all the good stuff to some of the bad. She's going to point out some flaws in your argument, or some baggy spots in your story, some language that fails to persuade, or some scenes that don't fly.

And if you react as most professional writers do, writers who take their craft seriously and have spent years honing it to a fine edge, you will scream bloody murder.

We know our work isn't perfect—but we don't believe it.

Even after all these years, it's still a shock to me that my manuscripts aren't camera-ready as they are. In fact, I just received, from the *Los Angeles Times*, an edited version of my upcoming essay, which now begins with what I regarded as my third paragraph. The first two are missing altogether. But guess what? Upon cold and grudging reflection, I can see that the piece didn't need those two paragraphs; now it starts with a declaration, rather than a mumble. (May I offer a trade secret? Most journalism begins with more of a preamble than it needs to. Since you're seldom sure where to begin, you start further back than you had to and kind of meander up to the starting line. Always look to see—as I should have done—that you're beginning at the most intriguing and appropriate spot.) The piece has also shed a few other sentences, like unwanted pounds, later in the piece—and it's leaner and meaner as a result.

Though at times it may not feel that way, editors really do have your best interests at heart. Not because they love you so much, but because your best interests and theirs neatly overlap. A book that gets bad reviews, or an article that draws negative letters to the editor, makes trouble for both of you. If you don't look good, to paraphrase the old Vidal Sassoon slogan, the editor doesn't look good. Her responsibilities are not only to you, but, in the case of journalism, to the newspaper or magazine she works for. She has to make sure that your work, no matter how unique, also conforms to all of the publication's own criteria. Does it suit their style? Is it their usual length? How does it fit into the issue or edition it's destined for? Will it work for their audience in its present state, or does it need tweaking? While you're your own boss, she might have dozens.

Which is why it behooves you to (a) squelch that scream, (b) listen carefully to what she's got to say, and (c) cooperate to the best of your abilities. I know so many would-be writers who have simply burned too many bridges by refusing to budge, or by squabbling over every edit. No, I'm not suggesting that you roll over and let your precious prose be steamrollered. But you must recognize, hard as it sometimes seems, that the edited draft *may be* an improvement over the original, that the editor may know a thing or two after all, and that sometimes the most important thing is to shepherd the present piece into print. That way, other pieces may successfully follow. An editor who isn't afraid to work with you—an editor who might actually enjoy working with you!—can be the best friend you've ever had.

RULE 87.

CHOOSE YOUR WORDS.

Okay, here's one for you history buffs. Did you ever listen to the Watergate tapes, secretly recorded by President Nixon in the Oval Office? I first heard them at the Richard Nixon Museum in Yorba Linda, California, but there are various websites now that also provide them. I was writing a magazine article about the presidential museums—and what struck me wasn't so much the substance of those private conversations—much of the time, it's almost impossible to follow—but the way that Nixon and his cronies communicated with each other. They spoke in broken sentences, elliptical phrases, grunts, vague allusions, offhand references, bits and pieces of what seem to be random notions and ideas.

But here's the weird part—those guys are following each other perfectly well. Despite the fact that they talk over each other, seldom complete a thought, interrupt, digress, evade, they are having what they consider to be an absolutely ordinary discussion. And it's working for them.

But if you were to quote dialogue like this, verbatim, in an article, your editor would figure you had lost your mind. She would expect you to do what we have grown to consider the unthinkable. She would expect you to edit the quotes.

Edit the quotes! you might say. *Isn't that a hanging offense?*

Not really. Journalists do it all the time, though we consider it more a matter of *cleaning up*, or even *massaging*, the quotes. As any reporter with a tape recorder can tell you, people only say what they mean in the most roundabout, garbled, indirect way. They use thirty words to say what they meant to convey in ten. They start one sentence—get distracted—then start another—then return, before they completely forget, to finish the first. Sometimes, for the reporter, it's a matter of divining their meaning—what they *intended* to say—from the word salad that they actually did utter. What counts, above all, is staying as true as is humanly possible to the gist and the import of their words. If, after the quote has been cleaned up and rendered halfway grammatical, it says what the subject was trying to express, then the reporter has done his job and acquitted himself in a professional manner. But making it *perfectly* grammatical, in the strictest sense, is also a question. What if your subject is an eloquent professor, who accidentally mixed up her tenses while musing aloud? Do you fix it? Probably. The idea, again, is to stay as close as humanly possible to the manner and idiom in which the person normally speaks.

But what if the subject is a little rough around the edges, someone who doesn't speak the King's English? Do you polish up his quotes, so that he comes off sounding more patrician, or do you try to convey—while not losing the sense of what he is saying—the idiosyncratic way he speaks? Again, you'd be wise to make the quotes hew to the general manner in which he comports himself. I remember once interviewing a crusty old farmer—he ran a date farm in the desert near Palm Springs—as part of a travel article, and when I asked him if his wife liked dates, he shook his head and said, "Nah—she got no use for the dang things." But when the article had been edited and appeared in the magazine, the farmer had suddenly become, I guess, the secretary of agriculture, because his answer to the question now was, "No, she doesn't enjoy dates." (Now that, my friends, is bad editing, and I doubt even the farmer recognized himself anymore.)

A good quote is one where your readers get the exact words, or enough of them, to understand the meaning and the tenor of your subject's remarks, and where even the subject believes that it's just what he said, and just the way he said it . . . dang it all.

RULE 88.

CHOOSE THEIR WORDS, TOO.

When it comes to writing dialogue in a story or screenplay, what's true for journalism holds true for fiction, too.

If you tried to emulate everyday speech *exactly*—the way that Nixon and his pals, for instance, used it—then you, too, would be scrambling your characters' thoughts all over the page, and leaving the reader to sort through the mess and extract some meaning.

But that's not what you do— and it's not what readers expect. When you write dialogue, you are re-creating the sound and the spirit and the shape of a verbal exchange, but you are automatically editing and refining it. You are focusing on the substance of the conversation, and bringing it out in a far less discursive, and far more defined, manner. A good writer is able to convey the natural rhythms of speech without putting down every *uh* and *well* and *oh*, and every thought without violating the vocabulary, or the integrity, of the character who is speaking. (You want your blunt old farmer to sound like a blunt old farmer.) On the page, the spoken word becomes the written word, and in so doing it changes. Not a lot, but enough. It becomes more focused, more succinct. A crystallization, if you will.

In fiction, dialogue has a whole range of purposes, most notably delineating your characters. Forget "you are what you eat"—"you are what you *say*," should be the fiction writer's mantra. Characters reveal themselves with every word they do, or do not, utter. And that's why the words of dialogue you choose to share with your readers are so important; each one is a clue to your character's attitudes and identity. Your dialogue should sound as immediate and unpremeditated as real speech, without all the boring stuff that usually smothers it like lumpy gravy.

Dialogue in a fictional context also has to move the story along—we have to learn something new, something potentially important, from each line or exchange. The reader assumes that's why the lines are there. You've promised a story, after all, not a transcript.

Nor did you promise to faithfully record every odd pronunciation or abbreviation common to some character's dialect. Writing in dialect, which many aspiring writers attempt, is in most cases a formula for disaster. Mark Twain could do it, but even he would have trouble getting it past an editor today—and not only because it's now considered politically incorrect. Dialect makes readers work harder than they generally want to work, and for the writer it's often difficult to get it on the page with any reliability. If this dialect angle is really important to you, just throw in a word or two, here and there, and leave it to the reader to supply, in his own head, the rest of the performance.

Finally, you might try a little drill I learned working in TV. Reading from the script, you were supposed to put your finger over the name of the character speaking, and then try to guess whose line it was. If you couldn't do it, then the line probably needed to be rewritten, in order to be more distinctive and more in keeping with the character who was supposed to say it. (Of course, most of the shows I worked on were so lame that they *had* no credible characters.) But you might try this technique with your own fiction—are the people speaking immediately identifiable? Or do they need a little more voice work before they fully come into focus?

RULE 89.

BEWARE OF EASY INSPIRATION.

It was a TV scene I was particularly proud of writing. A deranged man, afraid of supernatural forces, retreats to his room and feverishly papers the walls and windows with crucifixes and pages of the Bible.

The show's producers liked it, too. In fact, they told me they liked it when they first saw it, years before, in *The Omen*.

Which was when I, too, remembered seeing it there. Oops.

I should have guessed something was wrong when I wrote it—the scene came flying off my keyboard way too easily. I seldom get an idea that good so effortlessly, and script scenes aren't often that fully realized in my mind. Writing that scene I'd felt like I was totally in the zone.

And I guess I was in the zone. Only who knew it was someone else's?

We are all repositories of vast amounts of information, and a lot of that information is from books we've read, movies we've seen, stories we've enjoyed. We've absorbed it all, and when we write, some of it gets reprocessed. Of course, if it isn't reprocessed enough, it's called plagiarism. But if it is, it simply serves as a kind of fuel for our own imagination and the stories we then make up on our own.

But a warning bell should go off in our heads when something comes *too* swiftly. Yes, it might just be the fruits of a sudden inspiration . . . or it could be that we've accessed something we've already seen or read elsewhere. It could also be that what we've just written is a cliché, something so hackneyed and predictable that we wrote it with all the haste that countless others have written it before us. Sure it came easy—we didn't have to stop to do any thinking.

I once worked under a TV head writer who claimed you should throw away your first three versions of every scene, so that you could then get to that fourth, and truly original, version that you still had germinating inside you. Now, that man happened to be an idiot, and as far as I could tell, he should have been throwing away his fourth, fifth and sixth drafts, too. But there *was* a kernel of truth in what he said. That first draft of anything you write is often filled with easy beats, with the stuff that seems to spring, like Athena, full-blown from your brow. If a scene, a passage, a paragraph, did come to you with that kind of expedience, you might want to take a second look. It could be fantastic . . . or it could be recycled. Just take a moment to consider. I'm reminded of Samuel Johnson's oft-quoted, but dead-on, warning: "What is written without effort is in general read without pleasure."

RULE 90.

ADD A DASH OF METAPHOR.

Somewhere in our youth, we were all taught the inestimable value of metaphors and similes. If we weren't stuck in church, hearing about how "a mighty fortress is our God," we were in school learning from Shakespeare that the "quality of mercy . . . droppeth like the gentle rain from heaven." If we weren't with Wordsworth as he wandered "lonely as a cloud," we were discovering from Langston Hughes that dreams deferred dried up "like a raisin in the sun." No great writers—and that went double for poets—could go very long without comparing one thing to another, without holding up the metaphorical lantern to reveal some deeper significance in the ordinary, or, conversely, something mundane in the cosmic. Metaphor can inflate or deflate. It can bring something down to earth, and show it to us in a human dimension, or it can toss that thing toward the sky and show us how much bigger, and more meaningful, it is than we first thought.

It's like a telescope (to use a simile). Look through one end and things get smaller, look through the other and they get larger. Either way, you've got a new perspective.

That's what makes metaphor in general such a useful tool. You don't have to find plain, blunt, unmusical words to elaborate on something; you don't have to resort to explaining things like you're writing a computer manual. Instead, you can find colorful comparisons, or surprising equivalents, that wake up your readers, make them think, and reveal what they're looking at in a whole new light. Done right, a good metaphor can accomplish all that.

But done wrong, and that's what happens all too often, the metaphor can tangle up your prose, and your thoughts, in a fine web of confusion. (I think there's a metaphor in there.) Instead of shedding light, it casts a shadow, making something less clear and less comprehensible. For instance, you might easily compare a teeming airport to an ant colony—people would get it right away—but if you compared it to an overloaded library shelf, you'd probably have more readers scratching their heads in confusion than nodding them in agreement.

Beware of animals, by the way; they'll get you into trouble. Almost any common phrase you can think of that has an animal in it is both a metaphor and a cliché. (Two for the price of one!) No character in your work should ever be as happy as a clam, as sly as a fox, as greedy as a pig, as busy as a bee, as stubborn as a mule, as quiet as a mouse; nobody should ever eat like a bird, drink like a fish, stop like a deer caught in the headlights, or run around like a chicken with its head cut off. These are all as old as Aesop, and have just about as much life left in them.

There are those who have a gift for metaphor, and those who don't (including me). If you've got it, go to town; metaphor can enrich and invigorate anything from an editorial to a term paper. If you haven't got it, proceed with caution. Your words could wind up sounding as flat as a pancake, or cling to you like a cheap suit in the rain, or wither like fruit on the vine . . .

See? I told you I don't do metaphor well.

RULE 91.

RID YOURSELF OF *WRITING* WORDS.

I hate public readings.

Authors are generally terrible readers. They mumble, they get their own prose rhythms wrong, they're afraid to make eye contact. And that's only the half of it. (Oh, and they're bad dressers, too.)

But the real reason I hate readings is because most written words were never intended to be recited or performed. They were composed for the page, designed to accommodate, and even exploit, the peculiar but intimate communion that exists between the writer and the reader. They were crafted to echo in a head, not a lecture hall or meeting room.

Even the best writing—Doctorow's, Nabokov's, Updike's—writing that gives the language a thorough workout, often doesn't sound right when read out loud. In fact, I'd venture to say, it often sounds *more* wrong than cheaper prose does. Since we're not used to hearing such carefully wrought words recited, they assume a heightened artificiality. No matter how beautifully they adorn the page, or ring in our inner ear, at a reading they come off like somebody showing up at a clam-bake in wingtips and blazer.

And that's, as I said, the *good* stuff.

Lesser prose may, perversely, make for easier listening, but it's also less memorable and hardly worth listening to in the first place.

Furthermore, much of it is filled with words like *furthermore*—words that are written all the time, but seldom spoken. Add to that list things like *insofar, inasmuch, all told, nevertheless, nonetheless, hereafter, in future, moreover, with respect to, in terms of, at this point, on the basis of.* Just about any preposition or conjunction that has to mush together two or three words to do its job is a mush you don't need. Try a simple *since*, or *when*, or *to*, or *about,* or *if*; it'll usually get you where you need to go with a lot less trouble. While you're at it, use the terms *the former* and *the latter* sparingly. Why make your reader stop and back up, as I

invariably have to do, just to see which is which? Writing is a shark—
it must keep moving forward or die.

Knock off the "stand-in words," too. Say you're writing a piece
about a swamp, but you don't want to say swamp again, so the next
time you write "marsh" instead, and "bayou" the next, and "a silt-filled
squishy pond" after that. Before you know it, you're up to your waist
in mud, and the reader is trying to clamber out of the verbal morass as
desperately as you are. Despite the dangers of creating a verbal echo,
just say swamp.

Finally, avoid, abjure, and abstain from the editorial *we*. When *we*
opine, *we* had better be standing on a soapbox, delivering a speech on
world peace. And even then, we run the risk of getting hit with a well-
aimed, and well-deserved, tomato. *We* used to be reserved for royals,
and as far as I'm concerned, they can keep it. If you're not a king or
queen, and you're using it, you had better be suffering from multiple
personality disorder. Then you're entitled.

RULE 92.

CONVERT YOURSELF.

Recycling, I think we'd all agree, is a good thing.

If you write a piece of journalism, and you're able to sell it three or four times, more power to you. That's why things like First North American serial rights, secondary rights, foreign rights, etc., were invented.

But the raw material from which you write can also be recycled—and often is. That newspaper piece you wrote might contain the kernel of what could make a perfectly good short story. That short story might have the potential to be turned into a full-length novel. That novel may have such a strong, simple narrative line that it begs to be turned into a movie script. The subjects that have captured your imagination in the past are very likely to maintain their hold for some time afterward, and they may display a different, or even greater, power when expressed in a new medium.

But only if you can get out of your own way.

Since I have tended, lately, to go back and forth between scripts and books, I've had several friends ask for advice about the conversion process. They've written a novel they can't get published, or a screenplay they can't get produced, and now they want to take the story and recast it in another format. I see the logic, and I understand the impetus. I've been there myself. You've put all this energy into constructing a complete story, with a beginning, a middle, and an end, and you can't stand to let it all go to waste. It wasn't easy to get this far!

But if you find yourself in a similar situation, the first thing you have to do is take the original version of the story (whatever it is), read through it one more time, and then put it away. Put it in the bottom drawer of your desk, then close the drawer, and leave it closed. Lock it, if you can.

What you remember of the story is all you need.

You'll be tempted, I know, to keep opening that drawer, but every time you do, you will be pulled back into the previous version, and the story will never make a new life for itself in a fresh format. You'll make yourself crazy trying to find ways to replicate its every beat, every line of dialogue, every turn of phrase—and it cannot be done.

It cannot be done because a novel is not a movie, a movie is not a play, a play is not a short story. Every form has its own limitations and its own advantages—a novelist gets to use internal monologues, a screenwriter gets to skip long descriptions—and no story can survive intact the conversion from one form to the other. (Surely you've noticed how many good books make lousy movies.) What you have to do is reimagine the core material, and the only way to do that is by putting the first version out of sight, and out of mind. That way, the new form you're working in will have a chance of revealing to you all kinds of stuff that had never occurred to you the first time around, all kinds of opportunities for drama, humor, suspense, that either weren't there before, or that you couldn't access because of the strictures imposed by the format you were working in. (In a first-person story, for instance, you can't mention that the stalker just flitted, unseen, past the window—if your heroine didn't see it, your reader can't, either—but in a movie it's a natural, and you've just ratcheted up the audience's sense of danger, without yet alerting your protagonist. It's one of the oldest tricks in the screenwriter's play book.)

Converting a narrative is not a process of close transcription, much as you might like it to be. It's a process of re-discovery, of finding that original impetus or idea or story and recasting it in a whole new way. The best material, you'll find, can stand the test.

RULE 93.

PUNCTUATE THAT THOUGHT.

I once had a private writing student, an honors graduate of a prestigious, small college, and I'll never forget the look on his face when I returned a chapter of his novel to him with the punctuation corrected. *A lot* of the punctuation corrected.

"Yeah, okay," he said, glancing at all the little red marks. "Whatever." He shrugged, and gave me the look you might give a hopeless pedant. "Don't the publishers have people who worry about this little stuff?"

He was certain the book would be published very soon (even though this was only the second chapter), and when I tried to explain that this "little stuff" could keep it from getting that far, he looked at me as if I'd truly lost my mind. For him, punctuation was a trifling matter, beneath the notice of an *artiste*, and he certainly didn't want to waste any of our weekly conference time on it.

Frankly, neither did I. I was hoping he'd learned all this stuff back in high school, but as it appeared he had not, I had to give him a crash course in punctuation, and even more importantly, I had to explain why it *did* matter.

For one thing, errors in punctuation can quickly persuade editors you're not a professional, and that's often all the excuse they need to toss your manuscript into the wastebasket.

For another—and this was, to me, far more to the point—punctuation is such a critical tool that any writer who ignores it is nuts. It's like a chef deciding to cook without a spice rack, or a carpenter dispensing with his nails and screws. It's an essential part of what you have to work with, and it's not a hindrance, it's a help.

Dashes and hyphens, ellipses and semicolons, periods and parentheses—they seem, I know, like so many niggling little details (that's certainly what my writing student thought), but in fact they're the means to inject inflection and expression into your work. You can't *raise* your voice on paper, not literally, but an exclamation mark can make your intentions plain. You can't *lower* your voice on paper, not literally, but a parenthetical phrase allows you to slip in a sotto voce aside. A dash can do exactly what its name implies—pull your reader brusquely along—and a colon can bring him to a sudden stop. Commas—which seem to fall in and out of good repute—are like traffic cones on a highway, guiding your reader this way and that, around obstacles, into the next and safer lane. Personally, I love commas (which may be evident in this book) because I want my readers to hear the words exactly the way I do, in the same cadence I first imagined them.

But I'm not a total punctuation nut. I know that there are all kinds of highfalutin rules about the proper use of dashes versus hyphens, colons versus semicolons, etc., and I do recommend following these rules, if you can figure them all out. They're the rules of the game, and your readers generally expect you to play by them.

But to my mind, you, the writer, remain the higher authority—and if you want to bend the rules to suit your own purpose, to make the meaning of your work more precise or the rhythm more engaging, then go right ahead. That's actually what those pesky little punctuation marks were invented for—to help you make your writing voice as distinctive as possible. Think about them carefully, and use them freely, to convey the melody of your prose, like all those tiny notations on a musical score, as smoothly and as beautifully as you can.

RULE 94.

BUILD THE
PERFECT READER.

In many ways, building your perfect reader is like training a dog. For good behavior—like sitting still and paying attention—you offer rewards. For bad conduct—failing to turn the page, turning on the TV—you have to corral the wayward beast and once again regain its trust. A loyal reader is a writer's best friend.

But, to an extent seldom acknowledged, such readers have to be built from the ground up. Only with constant positive reinforcement and regular treats will your readers become, and remain, who you need them to be.

First of all, you have to grab them. They're wandering around, lost, lonely, in search of entertainment and/or edification. If your opening pages, or even your opening paragraphs, don't contain something striking, you may have lost your only chance of snagging them. It's a multichannel world we live in, and the mental remote is always in play.

In those same early passages, you must also give your readers a clear sense of what they're about to encounter. If you start out with a high-minded paean to democracy, they settle down in their chairs with their thinking caps on, prepared to absorb a valuable lesson in civics. If you begin with a casual anecdote about kids and car travel, then they're already primed for some smiles. The bait-and-switch technique, so beloved by used-car dealers, seldom works with prose—readers catch on quickly, and they can leave with equal alacrity. (After all, no one's looking.)

But readers respond to the writer even more than to the subject matter. If you start out with the right tone of voice—engaging, direct, intelligent—you can persuade them to come along for a ride they would never otherwise have taken. (I just read a long article about a rock 'n' roll roadie that captured me, against my better judgment, with its opening description of the guy's multiple tattoos.) If you're using humor, then deploy it quickly—why not let your audience know right off the bat that they're in for a few laughs? But don't go altogether crazy. The best comedians know when to let the audience breathe for a few seconds; they know that they have to spend a little time setting up the next big laugh.

Know, too, how to leave your audience. No, they don't have to be laughing (though that can be a good thing), but they do have to feel satisfied, rewarded. The ending of the article, essay, book, whatever, has to give them the sense that they've completed the journey, and that they've landed comfortably and intact. If they signed on for a luxury cruise, you don't want to heave them onto the wharf with a bad case of dysentery and a bump on the head.

Above all, love your readers—and they'll love you back. If you write in cringing fear, waiting for the critical brickbats, then your fear, and your resentment, will come through in the work. People will flock for the exits. But if you write with an amiable, fearless disposition—blithely confident of a fine reception—your own attitude will infect your readers. Do this enough, and you will eventually achieve what all of us who write most covet—an audience already attuned to us and our work, ready to laugh at our jokes, nod at our solemnities, and best of all, seek out and gobble up whatever we do next.

RULE 95.

DON'T BELIEVE EVERYTHING YOU READ!

Speaking of cringing in fear . . . I'd been living there a lot lately.

A few months ago, an industry trade publication—which has almost always looked favorably on my books—gave me the worst review of my life. An absolutely blistering piece by an anonymous critic, and even though I should have grown a thicker hide by now, I really went into a funk. I was so convinced that the book was terrible that I stupidly refused to do anything to advertise, promote, or publicize it, even (or especially) to friends. I felt like a dog who'd made a mess on the carpet and trembles at the thought of its owner coming home. I positively dreaded the impending publication day.

Well, guess what happened? A few weeks later, another industry publication called the same book "utterly captivating," and when it came out, it sold extremely well, and the aggregate reader reviews online were as high as any I had ever received before. Literally thousands of readers gave it five-stars (and these weren't all friends of mine) and my website was deluged with complimentary comments from readers all over the place. Many of them said that they couldn't wait to get hold of my previous books now.

What a fool I'd been.

Over the course of my career, with many books behind me, I've gotten great reviews, good reviews, and plenty of the most common breed—mixed reviews—but I guess I'd never been lambasted like that before. But the point is, I should have known, as my agent tried to counsel me, "that's just one person's opinion." I should never have let it convince me that my editors and publisher and agent were all wrong; they'd *liked* the book all along (but of course, I had discounted their opinions because they were already on my team).

Don't do that.

No matter what you write, you are going to have some fans, and some naysayers. Some lovers, and some haters. (Haters, in particular, thrive on the internet, as I hardly need to mention.) As long as you have done the work the best way that you can, then you can hold your head high. I'm not saying to ignore your critics—they may have a useful point now and then—but for God's sake, don't let them shake your confidence, impede your progress, or drive you to abandon your creations on the very eve of their debut—as I so recently did. You'd think I would know better, but there you have it. Many writers have fragile and teetering egos (mine is like an antique china teacup, balanced on a broom handle, atop a unicycle), but that's no excuse for letting the bastards grind you down. If they're such hotshots, let 'em try to write something of their own and then see how *they* like hearing from the peanut gallery.

RULE 96.

PASS THE SCALPEL.

Okay, let's say you've just finished reading something really terrific. A magazine piece so engrossing that you missed your bus stop, an essay that touched you more deeply than you would ever have expected, a book that you can't stop thinking about, long after you turned the last page.

Instead of just moving on, picking up something new to read or doing something else entirely, stop. Take that article, that essay, that book, and lay it out, as if on a lab table, for a lesson in gross anatomy. You can't call it a post-mortem—the thing is still alive—but you could call it a post-readem. Your goal? To figure out what the writer did to make his or her work such an affecting experience for you.

The first time through, you were caught up in the work, just letting it unfold and carry you along. But that's not what you're doing now. Now you're looking at it with a cold, critical eye—with an eye to dissect. You're looking for the secrets of its success. I think the first time I ever did this was when I was around ten years old, at summer camp, and I had just finished reading a James Bond novel. (*The Man with the Golden Gun*, if memory serves, but it could have been any one of them.) The climax had been painstakingly drawn out, and my preteen mind had been riveted for page after page. How, I wondered, had Ian Fleming pulled it off? Looking back over the last chapter or two, I saw that he'd cut away from the main action, gone off on another tangent for a few pages or paragraphs, and then returned again to the big chase. Just when you thought Bond's number was up, Fleming would divert your attention, and when you finally got back, something unexpected would happen to keep the drama cooking.

I tried it several times thereafter in my own stories, with varying degrees of success. But I never forgot the basic lesson.

Good writing achieves its effects almost invisibly; you don't see the strings, and you don't see them being pulled. Unless, of course, you look—and look hard. Ask yourself, *how did this essayist manage to draw me in so powerfully?* Did she reveal herself so honestly that you were irresistibly intrigued? How did she tell her story, or make her points, so effortlessly that you felt the power and the truth of what she had to say? Or, how did the book you were just reading use its shifting points-of-view to such advantage? (You should see my copy of a Scott Spencer novel, *Men in Black*, sometime [no relation to the Will Smith movie]; I couldn't believe how he'd managed to go back and forth between first person and third, in alternating chapters, and until I started diagramming the book, I hadn't even thought you were *allowed* to do that. I thought a committee of English teachers would descend on your house and arrest you.)

Wordsworth wrote that "we murder to dissect," and the guy had a point. But sometimes it's worth it. When you take apart and analyze a successful piece of writing, you get to see how the thing was put together, and why it worked its magic on you so well. If you're lucky, you'll also be able to capture some of that magic in your own work someday, and enthrall readers the same way that you were. What could be better than that?

RULE 97.

GATHER YE MOONBEAMS!

Want to know how to pick out the born writer in a grammar school classroom?

Look for the kid staring out the window, lost in space.

Writers are born daydreamers. It's not that we can't focus—we have to be able to do that in order to get any writing done—but our normal default state, the condition to which we will inevitably return, is one of unfettered free-association. Our thoughts, ungoverned, lead us in all sorts of directions, and we willingly follow. John Fowles once remarked that "in a novelist, a wandering mind is a good thing."

Some of our best ideas come to us in those aimless reveries, things that the logical mind would never have put together. The trick is catching these ephemeral notions, like butterflies in our net, before they flit away.

That's why many writers I know make a practice of getting out of bed, throwing some cold water on their face, and then immediately sitting down to work. They want to catch the loose, unedited, free-ranging liberty of the dream state. They want to hear only one voice in their head—their own true voice—without the distraction and the clamor that the rest of the day is sure to bring. What they don't do, ever, is turn on the radio or the TV, or even glance at the newspaper headlines. (What if something in the paper catches their interest?) In our dreams—the waking or the sleeping kind—we're as close as we're ever going to get to the fundament of our own minds. Freud said, "Dreams are the royal road to the unconscious," and whatever you may think about stuff like his notion of penis envy (I got over mine long ago), he was right about this. If you can get down to writing before you've lost all contact with your dreaming self, you may find a whole trunk loaded with material you would never otherwise have stumbled upon.

But maybe you're like me. Maybe you get out of bed only when and if the mattress has actually caught fire. And maybe you have to have

Alexa blasting classic rock just to find your way to the shower. Maybe it's noon before you begin to feel fully conscious. For you, like me, that early-morning routine may never get off the ground.

So try my alternative. Around my house, at eight thirty, nine o'clock at night, the phone stops ringing, the lights go down, the garbage trucks are no longer rumbling through the alleyway, and the doorbell isn't being buzzed by the UPS guy or the exterminator. Things settle down, and I settle down with them. Instead of catching the dream state after waking up, I catch it before going to sleep. If I'm at loose ends, with nothing much in the works, I let my thoughts roam. Writers are always getting accused of sitting around and doing nothing, when in fact doing nothing—or what *looks* like it—is useful and even necessary. (My ex-wife used to catch me at it and say, "Are you brooding again?" and only after I'd insisted, for the umpteenth time, that I wasn't brooding but *thinking*, did she learn to tiptoe around me at those times.) If I'm in the middle of some project, I nudge my mind in that general direction, and when I've finally gotten into the mood, and hit upon what I want to write next, I plunk myself down in front of the computer and go at it. Depending on your own sleep schedule, you might get in a good two or three hours of work before calling it a day—or night, to be more accurate—and rewarding yourself with a midnight snack. (Chocolate mint chip ice cream is usually mine.)

RULE 98.

LOSE YOUR PERSPECTIVE.

Years ago, when I was reviewing books, I was assigned a fat novel called *Weaveworld*, by Clive Barker—an immensely complicated story, it turned out, about a whole world of tiny creatures hidden in the fabric and pattern of a carpet.

And although my first reaction was, *What is this guy smoking?*—I soon found myself immersed in the tale and enjoying every minute of it.

What Barker, one of the most imaginative writers I've ever encountered, was able to do was draw me into that microworld and keep me there. And he was able to do it because he believed in it so passionately himself. Barker, whose body of work covers a vast range from flat-out horror to far-out fantasy, loses himself in the worlds he creates, and makes them so palpable his readers can lose themselves there, too.

When you write, as Barker does, any work of speculative fiction, you must somehow contrive to forget about all normal constraints and let the story lead you. You have to stop telling yourself, *This couldn't happen*, or *That never does*, and instead open yourself up to all the possibilities. It's no harder to type something fantastic than it is to type something ordinary.

It's really all a matter of perspective—and if you're willing to lose yours, the readers will lose theirs, too. When a piece of work is going well, you're immersed in the world of your own creating, you're lost in a universe where you are God and you can make up pretty much any rules you want. Time flows backward? *Fine.* There are five sexes? *Okay.* Animals talk? *Gotcha.* If you don't bury yourself, up to your eyeballs, in that world, you won't be able to write about it with any conviction or construct it with any solidity.

And yet, for most writers, there's always that little voice in the back of the head saying, *Are you crazy? Who's going to believe in something this strange?* (Such as a whole universe embedded in an old rug.) *Have you lost all perspective?*

No, what you've done is gain a *new* perspective, one that allows you to see a world where none existed, to tailor it to your own specifications, and function within its imaginary parameters. The only way to find such a place is to lose yourself there first.

LOSE YOUR PERSPECTIVE

RULE 99.

TAKE UP WHITTLING.

Most writers, when asked what they like to do in their spare time, first say *reading*, followed by some after-thoughts, like *going to the movies, riding a bike, taking long romantic walks on the beach at sunset.*

Usually, they're lying about everything but the reading.

Many writers, and I'm one of them, live in their heads. If you asked us why we even had bodies, we'd say it was so that we had something to cart our heads around. (Once, I checked out a local gym, and when I didn't sign up for the much-needed exercise classes, the buff blond salesman called me up the next week and said, "This is Brad—the voice of your conscience." "First of all," I told him, "I don't have a conscience, and if I did, it wouldn't be named Brad." Nor did I sign up for the exercise regimen.)

Some writers—and this mystifies me—like to spend their spare time doing crossword puzzles, or playing Scrabble. To me, those things seem way too much like work. Sitting in a chair, moving words and letters around, *for fun?* Not me.

But I do recognize the importance of finding an outlet, a hobby, something to distract you from the toil of writing. Many options present themselves—bungee jumping, Alpine mountaineering, spelunking—and all of them are fine choices, expressly because they don't involve words. (Bungee jumping may involve the occasional scream, but I don't think that counts.) What you need is a real holiday—not a busman's holiday—from the work you've been doing. If strenuous physical activity is as repugnant to you as it is to me, then you might try to find some other mindless, even monotonous, activity to indulge in— knitting, stamp collecting, jigsaw puzzles, whittling bars of laundry soap into perfect representations of your favorite classical composers. Winston Churchill made a hobby of bricklaying. The goal is simply to break the spell of words, if only for a few hours, that often holds writers in its grasp. You want your hands to be busy with something other than a pen or a keyboard—what better way to ward off carpal tunnel syndrome? And you want your thoughts—at least your conscious thoughts—to be focused on something other than the opening salvos of your editorial, or the dramatic conclusion of your play. Throw yourself into gourmet cooking, and you'll even be able to get dinner ready at the same time.

RULE 100.

SAVE EVERY SCRAP.

In the old days, before computers, it was a lot easier to hang on to your drafts. For one thing, typing was such a chore, comparatively speaking, that you were loath to toss out anything you had labored over. (You were also, sometimes, reluctant to make the small changes the piece really required; who wanted to type a whole page all over again just to add a neat phrase?) These days, of course, you just highlight whatever you don't like, hit Delete, and it's gone.

But most writers I know don't do that. Most of us either save those words we cut and drop them in a file somewhere, or we print them out and stuff them in a drawer—where, chances are, they will molder into dust. So why bother? For a host of reasons, only one of which I think is really critical.

Some writers believe in saving every word they write because they believe these words could come in handy later. Maybe they'll go back to a section of the piece, realize they should never have taken out the stuff they did, and be delighted to find that they can now just re-insert it. Waste not, want not.

There's also the chance that something they've edited out of one piece will work, later on, in something else altogether. A scene that doesn't play in one story may provide the jumping-off point for another; an argument that doesn't quite mesh with the rest of the book it's in right now might make a nicely contained essay for the *New York Times Magazine* later. All of it gets tossed into a file, a drawer, a cardboard box under the desk, there to live in hope of the final resurrection.

Which, to be honest, almost never comes. Most of the stuff you cut stays cut, and for good reason. It's very hard to take any portion of one manuscript and make it fit, with any success, in another. The more you try to fiddle, the more slippery and awkward the task becomes. You almost always wind up with what looks like a mannequin in an ill-fitting suit—lifeless and lacking in style. Apart, perhaps, from the inspiration provided by the original words, there's generally not a lot worth saving; you are better off just taking the gist of it and making something fresh and new. (And that's assuming you still have the interest in the material to do that, which isn't always the case.)

Still, with all of that said, I'll tell you the best reason for hanging on to every draft and every scrap of prose you write. And here it is. If you delete or throw something out, irretrievably, you will wake up in the dead of night convinced that the stuff you discarded is the best work you had ever done, that it was filled with priceless gems that you will never again be able to re-create or reimagine, and that you must have been mad not to see its extraordinary virtues at the time. You may even find yourself combing through your hard drive, or worse yet, climbing into a dumpster with a flashlight to try to retrieve the crumpled pages. (Ask me about that sometime.) Forget about the fact that you saw good reason to toss it at the time; now you'll think it was pure genius—unless, that is, you're again able to hold it in your hand, read it over, and say to yourself, *Oh yeah, that's why I got rid of it in the first place.*

ENGAGE IN NO FALSE ADVERTISING.

If you ask me, there are lots of bad ways to introduce an anecdote, but perhaps the worst is, "This is the funniest story you've ever heard."

Followed closely by, "You won't believe what I'm about to tell you."

For one thing, the story is never the funniest one I've ever heard (I tell those myself, thank you very much), and for another, I seldom believe what I'm told, anyway.

But what makes these intros so bad is that they set up expectations in the audience that will almost certainly go unfulfilled. If you start a story—either spoken or written—with a bold, over-the-top billing like that, you've raised the bar to an untenable height, and you've issued a sort of challenge to your audience. You've virtually *dared* them not to like what you're about to relate, and a lot of them, ornery by nature, will consequently put up some resistance. Since you told them how to react, they are now determined, on some subconscious level, to react differently, just to prove that they can't be pushed around.

This is not the right foot to get off on.

When you're writing, you're asking your readers to accept what you tell them. You're making a promise of sorts—that you will absorb, entertain, amuse, thrill, scare, amaze them. Your promise is implicit in every word you write, words intended to hold their attention and keep them avidly reading

But if you make that promise explicit—if you tell them what a great treat they're in for—then you'd better be darned sure you can back it up. If you can't, you'll have broken faith with your readers and they may decide, since they no longer trust you, to turn around and go home.

Every writer is, to some extent, a carnival barker, trying to lure the passersby into the tent. Lord knows there's a lot of stuff to read out there, and if you expect to snag someone's attention for very long, you've got to make a pretty persuasive case, and you've got to make it pretty quickly. But let the work speak for itself. Let the unfolding of your story, or the seductive quality of your prose, draw your readers in and, with luck, hold them there. Don't *tell* them how they're supposed to feel or react—just work your magic so that they *do* feel it.

RULE 102.

KEEP YOUR PROSE CLEAN.

The last thing I want to do is enter the current culture wars, especially on the conservative side of the aisle, but I do think it's worth saying a few words on the use of profanity.

First of all, using profanity, epithets, and coarse terms and/or dialogue in your work is, in my opinion, permissible and sometimes necessary. If you're writing in a freewheeling, discursive tone of voice, swinging for the bleachers, then go for it. We're all grown-ups here. If you're writing for a publication that offers a lot of latitude and a lot of attitude to match, then, again, be my guest. If you're writing an article about prison inmates, and this happens to be the way they talk, quote freely and verbatim. If you're writing a novel about Wall Street traders, whose language, in my experience, makes convicts sound like schoolmarms, show it (and them) for what it is. I've got no problem with using all the resources, and all the colors, of the language we've got. I'm not easily shocked, and neither are most readers, editors, and publishers.

But some are.

And that's why most writers err on the side of caution. It's not that they censor themselves—it's more that they maintain an awareness, however vague and inchoate, of their audience. When they write an article or essay, they keep the general public in mind. Would something they've written give offense? Would it appall a few prissy souls—or nearly everyone in the country? Is the use of the volatile stuff essential to the piece, or is it merely there for some kind of shock value or effect? And how much of it, honestly, is needed to make the point? If they're writing for a mass-circulation publication, most writers will take care to remain a polite neighbor to all the other writers and articles in the issue.

As with anything, profanity loses its power with overuse. The more a character, or a writer, swears and cusses, the more unremarkable the words become. That could be a good thing—maybe you're trying to inure your readers to a certain kind of world. But, overall, if you want to retain the curious impact of the "bad words," you have to parcel them out sparingly. That way, when you do elect to use them, they will still have the requisite wattage to rock your readers back on their heels, scorch the eyebrows right off their faces, or send them running for the smelling salts.

RULE 103.

DON A DISGUISE.

But okay, since I've just now put a foot into the culture wars, I'll put the rest of my foot.

We hear a lot these days about the crime of cultural appropriation— that is, when writers of one race, ethnicity, nationality, whatever, write about characters of another and in the process stake a claim to literary territory not necessarily their own. Jeanine Cummins, the author of the bestselling *American Dirt*, got into all kinds of trouble for writing a thriller whose protagonist was a Mexican bookstore owner, making the dangerous passage north. Although Cummins did years of research on the border, and wrote by most accounts (including mine) an absorbing story, she wasn't Mexican and, according to her many critics, had gotten a lot of things wrong.

That, of course, is a risk all writers run (and which the readers' comments thread on Amazon exists to remind you of. I have been raked over the coals many a time for historical bloopers.). But it's also a risk well worth taking. The beauty and the lure of writing fiction is the opportunity to imagine yourself into other times, other places, and, yes, other identities. If I were relegated to writing solely from my own life and experience, I'd be writing novel after novel about a Midwestern white guy, sipping cold coffee at his desk, with a cat draped, maddeningly, across his keyboard. Now there's a fast track to fame and fortune!

As a writer, your only responsibility is to tell the story as well, as movingly, and as *convincingly* as you can. And while solid research into your subject matter is of course essential, the real work is digging deep into your own humanity and drawing on that to flesh out the interior lives of your characters, no matter who they are, or how different their backgrounds may be from your own. Fortunately—and this is really a great break for writers everywhere—the whole range of human emotions is equally shared by all. Imagine that.

No less an authority than the Nobel Laureate Toni Morrison said that when she taught creative writing classes at Princeton University (my alma mater!), she expressly told her students *not* to write about their own family and friends, but to "think of somebody you don't know. What about a Mexican waitress in the Rio Grande who can barely speak English? Or what about a Grande Madame in Paris? Things way outside their camp. Imagine it, create it . . . I was always amazed at how effective that was," she said. "They were always out of the box when they were given license to imagine something wholly outside their existence. I thought it was good training for them." Later on, she added, "even if they ended up just writing an autobiography, at least they could relate to themselves as strangers."

What her lucky students were discovering was perhaps the greatest pleasure of writing fiction—the chance to enter and explore the world from other perspectives. Pulling it off isn't always easy—and these days it can get downright dicey—but the challenge is as irresistible as donning a Halloween costume was when you were a kid.

RULE 104.

PROTECT YOUR INSPIRATION.

There's no place like life to go for inspiration.

But it's not always that easy.

How exactly do you draw on the people, the incidents, the daily rounds of your own life without possibly exposing someone else's secrets, giving offense when you never intended to, or, worst of all, getting sued?

When you're writing, either fiction or non, you're pulling details, observations, thoughts, from a thousand different sources, most of them rooted in reality—*your* reality. Often, you're writing about friends and family members, you're writing about places you go, schools you've attended, events you've experienced, confrontations and conversations you've actually had. Those are the things that fill your creative well, as it were, and from which you're going to extract your article ideas, your stories, your vignettes.

If you're writing fiction—something that loudly proclaims itself to be *made-up stuff*—you have one easy out. If someone thinks she's spotted herself in one of your characters, and in an unflattering guise, you can always flat-out deny it. "You? Of course not. Why, I was actually thinking of someone I knew years ago, back in Akron." Or, the fallback position, "The character is a composite. It's no one in particular."

But, thankfully, this seldom happens, and for one simple reason. Most people think pretty well of themselves, and they never see themselves, as you or your narrator might, in an unfavorable light. Charles Dickens may have modeled Mrs. Nickleby on his own mother, but after Mama Dickens read the book, he says that she asked him "whether I really believed there ever was such a woman." I have a friend who's written a string of novels featuring some of the most horrendous wives imaginable, but he always covers his base by dedicating the books to his own dear spouse—who, so far at least, has failed to take umbrage, or initiate divorce proceedings.

In nonfiction, the trick is more difficult. This material is supposed to be true to life. Let's say you want to write a humor column about your Uncle Barney and his crazy get-rich-quick schemes . . . but Barney, as it happens, is still alive, he's still your uncle, and you're going to have to sit next to him at Thanksgiving. You don't want to hurt the old guy's feelings, but you know this is great material and you do want to use it. You can start, of course, by cleverly changing his name to Barry. And instead of making him your uncle, you can make him a neighbor. And instead of telling the story about his mushroom farming in the cellar, you can make up something else that never really happened. All of these alterations may help—Uncle Barney may not see himself in this oddball neighbor of yours—but the heck of it is, *you* may not see Uncle Barney in there anymore, either. You may have disguised him so thoroughly that you don't recognize the living, breathing character that inspired you in the first place. The power of the piece, which derived from the real Uncle Barney and your relationship to him, may evaporate in the process.

This is the conundrum that's a part of every writer's life. You can make the small concessions, but the more changes you make, the further you will get, inevitably, from the power source. All you can really try to do is preserve as much of life as you can, to stay a true as possible to the core of the experience, or the real person, you're writing about. If it winds up getting you in trouble, remember that you're in good company. The writer doesn't breathe who hasn't has to talk himself out of this tricky predicament at least once.

RULE 105.

MAGNETIZE YOURSELF.

Of all the afflictions that befall writers, dithering is one of the most common. Faced with seventeen different ideas, for everything from short stories to screenplays, many writers waste tons of precious time flitting from one to the other, wondering what to fully embark upon. It's so easy to start writing a novel, then hit an obstacle, and quickly decide that that short story idea looks much more promising, after all. Until that idea, too, hits a rough patch. When, suddenly, the stage play idea appears in a very appealing light. And so on and so forth, until weeks have gone by, and what you've finally got in the end is nothing but a bunch of false starts, first chapters, and opening scenes.

But once you do make a decision, and pick one project and stick to it, you'll notice something strange happens. (I don't know a writer who wouldn't second this.) You become a virtual magnet for related information and ideas. Suddenly, you will start discovering, all around you, all sort of juicy tidbits—observations, quotes, statistics, stories—that directly relate to, and nicely amplify, the project you're working on. You'll stop at a yard sale and find an old book, for 50 cents, which provides great background research. You'll turn on the radio and hear a song that's exactly what your heroine might be listening to in her big scene. You'll open the morning paper and come across a piece in the science section that neatly explains a rather arcane bit of business in your nonfiction tome.

The more you focus in on one piece of work, the more attuned you are to everything around you that might help. And there's *a lot*. Writers are scavengers—we find all kinds of odds and ends, and like birds building their nests we either paste them into what we're working on, or stash them away into notebooks for later use. (I am forever finding old magazine articles and newspaper clippings that I once cut out for reasons I can now no longer remember.) But when I'm immersed in one particular project, I am consistently amazed at the things that come to hand and that seem to have been tailor-made for me. If I weren't such a skeptic, I'd say there was a kind of divine providence behind it. (And I'd hate to think that God was spending time helping me with my thriller while famine, plague, and war afflicted countless millions.)

Whatever the mechanism behind it, once you choose a subject—or, as the case may be, let it choose *you*—you will soon discover that the world is behind you on this, and it'll start to provide you with a plethora of helpful bits and pieces, and sometimes even answers. If you don't mind my saying so, you've become a kind of black hole, a fixed, insatiable, and powerful force, sucking in everything germane that comes within reach. Into the bottomless hole it all goes, and while a real black hole never lets anything escape, in your case you do eventually release a book, a play, a movie script. Cosmologically speaking, that's a big advantage you've got there.

RULE 106.

SPILL YOUR SECRETS.

If you like paradoxes, try these.

Want to reach the broadest public? Go private.

Want to move your readers deeply? Think only of yourself.

Want to touch a universal chord? Focus on the intensely personal.

In the struggle to reach an audience, and connect with them in a powerful way, writers are forever trying to find the big topic, the big scene, the big, all-encompassing embrace. How, they wonder, can they make their own experiences more universal, how can they find a way to relate what they know and feel to what thousands, even millions, of other people may think and feel? How can they forge a bond between their own limited perspective and that of all these faceless, nameless readers that they are, nonetheless, desperately anxious to communicate with?

And the answer is simple.

It's not a matter of going wide—of trying to fill the biggest canvas, or paint in the broadest strokes. You don't have to wrestle with issues of war and peace, or in fiction with characters of epic proportion. Nothing has to be of immense or shocking scale. You don't have to raise a monument.

What you do have to do is *dig*.

Deep.

The more specific you become, the more generally felt your writing will be. The more revealing you are—of your own emotions, and thoughts, no matter how uncomfortable some of them may be—the more you will strike a chord in others. The more you are willing to examine yourself, honestly and openly, the more your work will speak to people you would think have nothing in common with you.

And the reason isn't so hard to come up with. We're all alike, in more ways than we'd like to admit, and we all have secrets that we think no one else could possibly share—doubts and fears that we think assail only us, shameful emotions and unspoken needs that we're sure consume nobody else, dreams and desires that we wouldn't confide even to our analysts. (Go ahead and admit it—it *killed* you when your best friend sold her book in two weeks! Or your old boyfriend found his next true love way before you did.) We're all a bundle of neuroses and insecurities, prevarications and procrastinations, slippery evasions, broken promises, and insincere avowals. The list goes on and on—and it's not pretty.

But it *is* true. And that's all that matters to you. Because if you, as a writer, can tell the truth, if you can really take the elevator down to your own sub-basement, and then come back up with what you found there, you will never want for a responsive audience. They'll be endlessly curious, and oh so grateful—so relieved!—to discover that there's someone else on the planet who's just as screwy as they are.

and just in case you're wondering, if I ever write Tell the Bride about camera shy with the red dress was later retitled The Teenage Cleaver Go Apply and Ale Hype. We should all have it have browneies that good.

RULE 107.

HIT THE
SNOOZE ALARM.

Around four o'clock every afternoon, I take a break from writing, in order to do one of two things—take a walk, or take a nap.

The walk helps to clear my head, open my lungs, raise my heart rate, limber up my muscles, improve my mood, burn calories, and enhance my social skills (should I bump into some other aimless soul).

That's why I usually opt for the nap.

But to be done properly, a nap must adhere to certain long-established practices and procedures. For instance, to qualify as a nap, and not as going to sleep or knocking off altogether, a nap must be taken on a sofa, or in a chair, or on any other flat surface *not* a bed. No sheets and blankets, no fluffy down pillows, no orthopedic mattress. There has to be a hint of the temporary about it, even if that brings with it the smallest element of discomfort. For instance, I usually nap in my old wingback armchair, with my head twisted to one side, my feet on a rickety ottoman, and my chest warmed by a spread-out section of the newspaper. (Please, for your own sake, do not try to picture this.)

Duration of the nap may not exceed forty-five minutes, after which, again, it would now officially qualify as sleep and thereby subject you to arrest.

But here's the great thing about it—those naps can be not only refreshing, but even productive. Your mind is constantly working on multiple tracks at once, and many is the time that I, like many a tortured artist, have arisen only to discover that a problem has been solved or an issue settled while I was ostensibly just napping. I crawl back to my desk with a fresh eye, and might wonder why I had thought myself so snagged in the first place. Robert Louis Stevenson even went about it in a more organized way. He had what he described as his army of little brownies, and he would give them their marching orders before he shut his eyes. Their job was to bring back a marketable story idea, and just in case you're wondering if it ever worked, the brownies came back with the tale that was later entitled *The Strange Case of Dr. Jekyll and Mr. Hyde.* We should all have brownies that good!

RULE 108.

CALL IT QUITS.

Writing is all about perseverance. No question about it. It's all about dedicating yourself to the project at hand, and, whatever the obstacles, seeing it through to completion.

But it's also a matter of knowing when to quit.

Sometimes, you're going to have a bad idea. Or, you're going to start on something that just plain doesn't work. Or that fails to take off in the way you hoped. Sometimes, in short, you're going to lay an egg.

When is it fair, when is it wise, to throw in the towel on work that isn't working? There are lots of things militating *against* the decision. For one, you've already put in all this time and effort, writing thousands of words that will now languish in obscurity. Economists and accountants have a term for this—I think it's "sunk cost." You want *some* return on your already sizable investment, even if it means investing more.

But you won't necessarily get it.

Nor do you want to think of yourself as a quitter. Don't all the writing books and teachers advise you not to give up, to keep on plugging? Don't they all tell you that these sloughs of despond are only natural and nothing to worry about?

True enough, but sometimes your unshakable misgivings and increasing doubts are valid; they're telling you something. What's important is to listen carefully. They're not, for instance, telling you that you're a worthless writer. They're not telling you that you're a quitter. They're not telling you that you will never write again.

They're simply telling you that this one thing, this one project, isn't going anywhere. That even you have lost interest in it for some reason. And if it's not holding your own interest any longer, how can it ever be expected to grip a reader? In two words, it can't.

There isn't a professional writer on earth who hasn't had to abandon an essay, a poem, a novella. But that didn't stop them from starting on something else. Sometimes these abandoned projects serve as the necessary corrective, the false start that points the way to the true one. Sometimes they're a liberating exercise, a sneeze that had to be released.

And sometimes they're just clunkers. Don't be mad at them; don't be mad at yourself. Just quietly chalk 'em up to experience, and move on.

But as I said in an earlier rule, *never* torch every remnant. I was once working on a novel that had stalled and I'd consigned the incomplete manuscript to a banker's box in my closet. Well, about a year later, my whole life stalled, and in a far worse way. I was in a weird accident, and for the better part of a year I was out of commission. And when I was trying to make my comeback, what should I happen upon—while rummaging in my closet for an old space heater—than that banker's box. To my own surprise, what I'd written seemed better than I'd remembered it, and when I showed it (with many apologies) to my agent, she said, "If you finish this, I can sell it. I promise." Taking her at her word, I wrote the rest, and yes, she proved to be right. I didn't get rich, but I did get back on track, and sometimes that's all it takes.

RULE 109.

GRANT YOURSELF
A TITLE.

Some writers are great at it; some (like me) stink. But if you think that you can slap any old title on your work and then send it out, you're making a big mistake.

And missing a big opportunity.

Your title is the first thing an editor, a publisher or your readers are going to see, and it tells them a lot about what's coming. If you write an article and put a silly, lighthearted title on it—"The Ten Worst Pick-Up Lines of All Time"—it tells them they're in for a breezy (and possibly pointless) read. If you write a book with what I think of as the "high colonic" title—*The History of the Whole World: An Eschatological Approach to Everything That's Ever Happened*—then they know it's time to buckle their seat belts. (Colons show up in many nonfiction titles, and almost invariably in books from academic presses, where the author has to make sure the subject sounds sufficiently weighty, obscure, and intimidating.) Your title is the banner that brings customers into your store, so make it bold, colorful, clever, provocative, mysterious, controversial, funny, intriguing, *anything*—just don't make it boring.

If you have trouble coming up with a title, that alone can also serve as a very helpful warning sign. It may signal a deeper problem with the project you've been working on. Whenever I've written, say, a humorous essay (or what I think *passes* as a humorous essay), and I can't come up with any title at all that seems to fit the piece, it usually means the piece hasn't really congealed as it should have. The more I cast about for a title that speaks to the point of the piece, without coming up with anything, the more I realize that maybe, just maybe, the piece doesn't *have* a single, clear point. Maybe it's grown too diffuse, or it rambles around over too much ground. What did I think was so funny about it in the first place?

By the same token, sometimes it helps to come up with a working title in advance. You can always change it, of course, but if you're worried about going off track, or forgetting the original impetus for the piece at hand, a working title can serve as a kind of lodestone, keeping you pointed in the right direction. It can also give the work a sense of solidity in your own mind—you're not just writing any old thing, you're writing *My Love Life,* the steamy memoir of your many escapades.

Novels, screenplays, and plays are a nightmare for titling. Chances are, they're about many things—they've got characters, plots, themes (buried and/or blatant.) With all of that to encompass, how, and what, do you fix on? And haven't all the good titles already been taken? (One of the many advantages of an Amazon.com world is that you can quickly check your title ideas against whatever is already out there.)

For inspiration, lots of writers turn to the same sources—*Bartlett's Familiar Quotations* and the Bible are probably the top two. You're looking for short, pithy phrases and expressions—sometimes they're good just as they are, sometimes they need a little tweaking. A title with a Biblical provenance (*The Sun Also Rises*), or a poetic one (*Tender Is the Night*) lends a classy tone to any project. Looking for just that sort of thing for one of my own novels, I kept coming up empty handed— until I decided to do some reverse engineering. I composed my own snatch of fake fifteenth-century verse, credited it in the book's epigraph to an anonymous poet, then lifted the few words I needed from it to give myself a decent title.

Am I proud of this behavior? No. But I can't say that I'm all that ashamed of it, either. There are few things in this world more desperate than a writer with no title to stick on his cover. (And I guess I did a pretty convincing job of it, since an eager grad student in Renaissance studies got in touch with me to find out more about the poem and its anonymous scribe.)

RULE 110.

LOVE WORDS.

In 1968, the poet Marianne Moore was giving a reading and when she offered to field some questions, someone in her audience asked her what advice, if any, she would give to an aspiring poet "who hates words."

After thinking about it for a few seconds, Moore said, "That may be very auspicious. Words are a very great trap."

With all due respect to Marianne Moore, who won the Pulitzer and the National Book Award and was in fairness probably just trying to be polite, that was the wrong answer! The questioner was probably just showing off—"Look at me, a poet who hates words! Is that deep or what?"—but if it was more than that, if the questioner really and truly hated words, then that's when Moore should have suggested a career in cosmetology.

Writers *love* words, or at least the real ones do. Oh, they may get plenty mad at them at times, the way you do at a family member who disappoints you in some way. (The worst injuries are the ones your loved ones inflict.) But words are all you have to work with, and when they don't come easily, when they don't sound on the page the way they did in your head, it can be the most frustrating thing in the world. You know what you *wanted* to say, you *thought* you knew how you wanted to say it, but those darn words you've just typed are somehow missing the essence of it. So, you have to strike them out and try again.

And then, who knows? You may have to cross them out all over again, after that.

Each time, you may come a little closer to what you want—to the scene you see in your mind's eye, to the argument you want to make, to the sentiment you wish to express—but the words aren't yet there. You still have to rummage through your toolbox for the right combination of nuts and bolts, to nail down the thing you envisioned.

And that toolbox holds every word you've managed to accumulate over the years . . . years of living, years of listening, and years of reading.

All the words you've overheard in supermarket lines and subway cars. All the words you've read on cereal boxes and billboards, in comics and classics, in blogs and classroom texts. (Writers read *everything*.) All the words you've spoken, in passion and in anger, all the words you've had thrown right back at you. If you don't love words, if you don't love what they can do, and how they sound in the right combination, and the infinitesimally different shades of meaning among them then, like Marianne Moore's questioner, you ought to look into another line of work. (And if English—one of the richest, most varied, and universally-known languages—happens to be your native tongue, then you're in extra luck!)

Writers wallow in words like pigs in a mud puddle, and the dirtier we get, the happier we are.

RULE 111.

BREAK THE RULES.

Yes, yes, how else could I end this book except with a plea to ignore rules and anyone with the nerve to make them?

Rules are made for breaking.

For example, for every writer who writes in the morning, there's one who writes only at night.

For every writer who plows ahead, never looking back, there's one who agonizes over every word and cannot go forward without polishing every syllable that has come before.

For every writer who works from an elaborate outline, there's one who flies by the seat of his pants. (In the business, such writers are sometimes referred to, unsurprisingly, as "pantsers," as opposed to "plotters" or "planners.")

Successful writers are always being quizzed. What computer program do you use for your screenplays? How did you come up with the idea for that novel? How long did it take you to write it? How much were you paid for it? How do you feel about reviews? Do you read the bad ones? What are you working on next? How do you get started? How do you know when you're done?

Implicit in all the questioning is the notion that there's some secret to the writing life, some way of working that professionals know—and privately share—and that amateurs suffer from not knowing. And the only real secret is that everything works—for somebody. Finding out what works for you is all a matter of trial and error. Are you writing the first draft of your book in longhand, on a legal pad, while sitting in a rocking chair? If it works for you (as it has for me), then that's your secret. Or, are you working on your laptop, on the crowded commuter train to the office? If the work gets done, then that's all you need to know.

At every public event I do, I get asked, as most writers do, something about inspiration, and about why I write. Usually I brush it off with some dumb joke about the mortgage payment being due, or by quoting that famous old saw of Samuel Johnson's: "No man but a blockhead ever wrote except for money." I even stuck that quote on one of my books, years ago, as the epigraph—and I've always regretted it. Why? Because I didn't believe it then, not really, and I don't believe it now. If I were that interested in money, I'd have gotten a real job years ago, or at least figured out just what the hell a hedge fund is.

I write, as most writers do, for other reasons. I write, to be painfully honest about it, because I want to be noticed, to separate myself from the herd. I want to be taken into account, and to have people hear what I have to say, even if it's only in a fictional context. At the same time, I feel like there's a big public debate going on all the time, all around me, everywhere from the news channels to the bookstore shelves, from Twitter to Amazon, and I simply can't bear to be left on the sidelines. Never could.

For all of us who choose to sit down and confront that scary blank page, writing is a way to enter into the permanent record everything from our transitory thoughts to our very existence, and no matter how modest we may claim our aims to be, on some level we're doing it for posterity. We want to see our book on a library shelf, our movie up on the big screen, or hear our lyric sung from a stage. We write in the unspoken hope that we, and our work—whether it's a novel or a script, a memoir or a monograph—will endure and become part of the passing parade that was our time.

As goals go, I ask you, how in the world could you do better than that?

THE END

ABOUT THE AUTHOR

Robert Masello is an award-winning journalist, television writer, and the best-selling author of both novels and nonfiction books.

His articles, essays and reviews have appeared often in such diverse publications as the *Los Angeles Times, New York Magazine, Newsday,* the *Washington Post, Redbook, Travel + Leisure, Harper's Bazaar, Glamour, Elle, TV Guide, Town & Country,* and the *Wilson Quarterly.*

His novels, published by many of the major houses and translated into nineteen languages to date, include, among others, *Blood and Ice, The Romanov Cross, The Einstein Prophecy, The Medusa Amulet, The Night Crossing, The Jekyll Revelation,* and most recently, *The Haunting of H. G. Wells.*

In addition to various TV shows and specials, he has also written for many popular series, such as *Sliders, Early Edition,* and *Poltergeist: The Legacy,* which have aired on CBS, NBC, UPN, Fox, Syfy, and Showtime.

An honors graduate of Princeton University, where he studied writing under Geoffrey Wolff and Robert Stone, he has since taught and lectured at such esteemed institutions as New York University, Chapman University, UCLA Extension, and the Columbia University Graduate School of Journalism. For six years, he served as the Visiting Lecturer in Literature at Claremont McKenna College, in Claremont, CA.

Today, he lives and works in Santa Monica, California.

Books from Allworth Press

Allworth Press is an imprint of Skyhorse Publishing, Inc. Selected titles are listed below.

Author's Toolkit, Fourth Edition
by Mary Embree (5 ½ × 8 ¼, 192 pages, paperback, $16.99)

Branding for Bloggers
by Zach Heller (5 ½ × 8 ½, 112 pages, paperback, $16.95)

Business and Legal Forms for Authors and Self-Publishers, Fourth Edition
by Tad Crawford, Stevie Fitzgerald, and Michael Gross
(8 ½ × 11, 176 pages, paperback, $24.99)

The Business of Writing: Professional Advice on Proposals, Publishers, Contracts, and More for the Aspiring Writer
Edited by Jennifer Lyons; foreword by Oscar Hijuelos
(6 × 9, 304 pages, paperback, $19.95)

The Fiction Writer's Guide to Dialogue
By John Hough, Jr. (6 × 9, 144 pages, paperback, $14.95)

Promote Your Book: Over 250 Proven, Low-Cost Tips and Techniques for the Enterprising Author
by Patricia Fry (5 ½ × 8 ½, 224 pages, paperback, $19.95)

Propose Your Book: How to Craft Persuasive Proposals for Nonfiction, Fiction, and Children's Books
By Patricia Fry (6 × 9, 288 pages, paperback, $19.99)

Publish Your Book: Proven Strategies and Resources for the Enterprising Author
by Patricia Fry (6 × 9, 264 pages, paperback, $19.95)

Starting Your Career as a Freelance Writer, Second Edition
by Moira Anderson Allen (6 × 9, 304 pages, paperback, $24.95)

Starting Your Career as a Freelance Editor
by Mary Embree (6 × 9, 240 pages, paperback, $19.95)

The Writer's Legal Guide, Fourth Edition
by Kay Murray and Tad Crawford (6 × 9, 352 pages, paperback, $19.95)

To see our complete catalog or to order online, please visit *www.allworth.com*.